Retrospective Conversion: History, Approaches, Considerations

Retrospective Conversion: History, Approaches, Considerations

Brian Schottlaender, MLS
Editor

The Haworth Press, Inc.
New York • London • Norwood (Australia)

Retrospective Conversion: History, Approaches, Considerations has also been published as *Cataloging & Classification Quarterly*, Volume 14, Numbers 3/4 1992.

The Haworth Press, Inc. 10 Alice Street, Binghamton, NY 13904-1580 USA

Library of Congress Cataloging-in-Publication Data

Retrospective conversion : history, approaches, considerations / Brian Schottlaender, editor.
    p. cm.
    "Has also been published as Cataloging & classification quarterly, volume 14, number 3/4, 1992" – T.p. verso.
    Includes bibliographical references.
    ISBN 1-56024-328-7 (acid free paper)
    1. Retrospective conversion (Cataloging) I. Schottlaender, Brian.
Z699.35.R48R48   1992
025.3'173 – dc20
                                           92-19493
                                              CIP

Retrospective Conversion: History, Approaches, Considerations

CONTENTS

CONTROL ISSUES

∞ ALL HAWORTH BOOKS & JOURNALS
ARE PRINTED ON CERTIFIED
ACID-FREE PAPER

Retrospective Conversion: History, Approaches, Considerations

ABOUT THE EDITOR

Brian Schottlaender, MLS, is Assistant University Librarian for Technical Services at the University of California at Los Angeles where he has coordinated projects resulting in the retrospective conversion of over one and a half million bibliographic records. From 1986 to 1988, Mr. Schottlaender served as the RTSD Co-Chair of the American Library Association's LITA/RTSD Retrospective Conversion Interest Group. He is currently a member of the American Librarian Association's Committee on Cataloging: Description and Access (CC:DA) and a candidate for the position of Vice-Chair/ Chair Elect of the ALA's Cataloging and Classification Section. Previously, he held cataloging positions at Indiana University and at the University of Arizona, where he was also coordinator of the Wright American Fiction Project.

Introduction

Brian Schottlaender

The American library community has been actively engaged in converting its manual cataloging records to machine-readable form since the mid-1970s. A lot of progress has been made; a surprising amount of work still remains to be done. Some institutions have finished (not many); others have not yet begun. Hence, retrospective conversion remains a timely topic.

An attempt has been in the arrangement of the articles to go from the general to the specific back to the general. While the articles comprising the two middle sections describe specific situations and projects, each includes a wealth of generalizable information.

Methodological options for retrospective conversion (recon) might seem myriad in number; in fact, there are essentially only three. One can either carry conversion out in-house, contract it to a vendor, or, more often than not, some combination of the two. Each option has advantages and disadvantages related to cost, staffing, time, and record quality. When authors have described workflows in their papers, as many have, they have been careful to discuss the relative advantages and disadvantages of each.

The aim of recon, of course, is the creation of a complete catalog in machine-readable form. Whatever option for achieving this aim is settled upon, the process will prove labor-intensive and expensive. As Bill Potter notes, "It should only have to be done once."[1] Therefore, the bigger the investment in advance planning, the better the eventual result. Each of the authors attends to this need for planning; the two authors in the final section concentrate on two of the costliest planning issues: quality and authority control.

These articles might easily have been subsumed under a different subtitle. The one selected, it is hoped, is both descriptive and succinct.

The first section, "History," begins with a detailed bibliography and review of the recon literature published between 1980 and 1990. Among many other topics, the 200+ items assembled and reviewed address general considerations, special formats, and international recon issues. The section concludes with Susan Vita's description of the conversion, under contract, of the Library of Congress' huge PREMARC file and strategies being explored by the Library for file cleanup.

While the two middle sections could all have been subsumed under the general rubric "Approaches," I have elected to arrange them more specifically. The articles in section two, "Case Studies," describe conversion projects at two specific institutions: one, a medium-sized academic library; the other, a large one. One project focussed on non-serials; the other, on serials. Each institution used several different approaches to complete its conversion project. When paired however, the articles serve to demonstrate that as disparate as institutions and projects may be, the issues and considerations in recon remain constant.

The third section, "Coordination and Innovation," again comprises articles describing several specific projects at specific institutions. Koth and Green describe seven different projects to convert music scores, widely recognized as amongst the most difficult materials to convert. This article includes specific and detailed descriptions of varying approaches to contending with the scores format, as well as a useful description of a carefully coordinated attempt at conversion amongst several institutions, under the auspices and leadership of the Associated Music Libraries Group. Sandore's article, like those in section two, is highly specific to a particular institution. It is distinguished, however, for its careful and detailed description of an unusual, and perhaps unique, PC workstation interface developed to facilitate the conversion process. In addition, the author describes the use of sampling techniques in project cost analysis.

The articles in the fourth and final section, "Control Issues," are perhaps more prescriptive than those in the earlier sections. The first takes the need for quality standards in recon as a given, focussing on "What standards?" and "At what cost?" In the course of his bibliographic essay, Lentz reviews quality control issues attendant upon general and special materials, types of cost, and levels of cost, concluding that editing and, perhaps more importantly, editing decisions are critical to the recon process. Maccaferri adopts a similar position and argues that authority control is as important in an online catalog as in a manual one, if not more so. He elaborates on the problems inherent in authority control in a recon context and on approaches to achieving various kinds and degrees of such control. The thread throughout his presentation is the need to define general authority control quality standards before one can devise similar definitions specific to retrospective conversion.

This volume results from the efforts of many. First and foremost amongst these, of course, are the authors themselves, without whose thoughtful and thought-provoking papers there would indeed be no publication. Ruth Carter provided both encouragement and guidance. In addition, she–and The Haworth Press, Inc.–showed remarkable patience. Kathy Marshall, my administrative assistant, helped at every turn with many of the details. Finally, my wife Sherri, as always, gave me the support only she can. Without them, this would not have reached fruition. To them then, the credit; to me, of course, full responsibility for any typos or other editorial mishaps which may have crept in.

NOTE

1. Potter, William Gray. The Evolving Online Catalogue in Academic Libraries. In Gorman, Michael and Associates. *Technical Services Today and Tomorrow.* Englewood, CO: Libraries Unlimited, 1990. p. 161.

Recon Road Maps:
Retrospective Conversion Literature, 1980-1990

Daphne C. Hsueh

SUMMARY. This paper aims to bring together in one place books, articles, reports, and lectures on retrospective conversion in print and non-print formats, appearing between 1980-1990. The bibliography, preceded by a brief review of the literature, is divided into ten broad categories to facilitate quick reference.

In these days of automation, no two words elicit stronger love-hate responses among technical services librarians than those in the phrase, "retrospective conversion" (recon). Love, because of the prospect of the promised land–an integrated system that will facilitate all aspects of library services to enhance information delivery. Hate, because of the horror of opening up a Pandora's box of old cataloging inconsistencies and idiosyncrasies, in addition to the seemingly endless tasks of record conversion and clean-up. There-

Daphne C. Hsueh is Retrospective Conversion Librarian and special assistant to the Head of Cataloging and is currently the Acting Chinese Studies Librarian at the Ohio State University.

fore, those who are suddenly thrust into the dubious limelight of planning and supervising a recon project deserve both sympathy and assistance.

For assistance one logically will go to *Library Literature* in search of any help in mapping out the whole path. There, one may be surprised to discover that "Retrospective Conversion" does not appear as a subject category until 1988. Prior to that time, there was "Retrospective Cataloging *see* Cataloging–Recataloging." Although "Retrospective Conversion" became a legitimate heading in 1988, the cross reference: "Retrospective Cataloging *see* Retrospective Conversion" remains.

This seemingly interchangeable usage of "Retrospective Conversion," "Retrospective Cataloging" and "Recataloging" in *Library Literature* is certainly a disservice to the recon manager who has to formulate the philosophical underpinnings of any recon project by clearly defining what retrospective conversion means to the library community he/she serves.

Fortunately, the literature as a whole does not share this confusion. Bryant and Beaudiquez (1990) come out most unambiguously in separating retrospective catalog conversion, retrospective cataloging and retrospective bibliography as three distinct activities. As a matter of fact, most writers warn of the danger of viewing a recon project as an opportunity for recataloging or upgrading a bibliographic record. The impact which the debate about conversion vs. cataloging can have on a recon project can be seen clearly in Card's (1984) description of the cooperative project to convert serials from UCLA, UC Berkeley, and Stanford.

The body of literature on retrospective conversion has grown steadily since Hogan (1986), which lists fifty-nine entries covering 1983-1986 and serves as a supplement to *Automation in Libraries: a LITA Bibliography, 1978-1982*, Carter and Bruntjen (1983), and Reed-Scott (1984). For the past few years there has been a marked increase in articles (plus one new book) on the general issues of retrospective conversion as compared to the "How-we-do-it-at-our library" type of article. Although reports on individual projects serve the purpose of illustrating how individual libraries tackle the enormous recon problem in specific settings, a novice to the field of recon needs the kind of detailed explanations and guidance available in works on a level close to that of a textbook. Therefore, one is happy to find Carter's classic work on data conversion (1983) supplemented by Beaumont's (1989). Kallenbach's presentation (1983), Reed-Scott's articles (1983 and 1985), and Epstein's three-part article on retrospective conversion revisited (1990) are among the many welcome additions to the general literature on recon.

By contrast, articles on the fine art of sampling for the purpose of a recon project are extremely scarce. All writers on the basics of recon stress the importance of knowing one's own collection because such knowledge is critical in determining both the size and the method(s) of conversion, in estimating the costs, in helping the vendor, if one is chosen, to calculate the bid, and in projecting the necessary time required. However, there are only two articles on sampling studies during these ten years that are specifically related to recon, though Dougherty's (1982), while for general library application, is extremely easy to understand. Clearly, more works on this important aspect of recon are urgently needed.

Articles on standards, guidelines and quality control, though a bit more numerous than those on sampling, are still not sufficient to cover these important aspects of a recon project. The U.S. came up with *proposed* guidelines developed in connection with an ARL study with Reed-Scott as the project coordinator ("Guidelines . . . ," 1985) while the Europeans, a bit more assertive, published bibliographic standards for recon (Sule, 1990). As to the issues of quality control in a recon project, there are only Miller (1984) and Juneja (1987) in the past ten years, although Carter and Bruntjen, early in the decade, state that the concept of main entry might have lost its importance in an online environment but the same is not true with regard to the concept of authority (1983, p. 10).

In a similar situation, the number of articles on how to prepare cost estimates is woefully few. What have been published are either cost analyses of a specific technology such as CD-ROM (Co, 1988 and 1990) or those which argue for a different method of distributing funds (Ra, 1987). These are articles of substance but a novice to a recon project certainly needs more help.

By contrast, articles written about various products and vendor services are in abundance, covering almost all available choices. Most articles deal with one library's experience with a product or a vendor. This is certainly helpful for people to understand how some of the products such as LaserQuest and CD-CATSS work.

In the category of different formats and special types of materials, serials, understandably, become the main focus. One is happy to find a few articles dealing with conversion of government publications and even with map conversion. However, there is, regrettably, not a single article on the conversion of analytics nor one on monographic series. The literature of recon of music scores and sound recordings is also sparse.

The publication of the *IFLA Journal* special issue on retrospective conversion (February 1990) places recon issues in an international context. One is suddenly aware of the added dimension of a bilingual catalog (Delsey, 1990) and the related issue of dual but connected authority control within a single database. This might give one the sense that problems in a mono-lingual catalog are not that bad after all.

The following bibliography does not claim to be exhaustive. It is compiled to help librarians who are embarking on a recon project to locate in one place some useful reading materials. Since no two collections are alike and no two libraries have the same cataloging practices even in these days of networks and shared cataloging in bibliographic utilities, it is only logical that there will never exist a blueprint of retrospective conversion applicable to all libraries. This body of literature on recon can only serve as a road map for one to find his/her own way.

GENERAL AND GENERAL SPECIAL

Adler, Anne G. and Elizabeth A. Baber, eds. *Retrospective Conversion: From Cards to Computer*. Ann Arbor: Pierian Press, 1984.

Asher, Richard E. "Retrospective Conversion of Bibliographic Records." *Catholic Library World* 54, no. 4 (Nov. 1982): 155-161.

Avram, Henriette D. "Retrospective Conversion: a National Viewpoint." *IFLA Journal* 16, no. 1 (February 1990): 55-57.

Avram, Henriette D. "Toward a Nationwide Library Network." *Journal of Library Administration* 8 (Fall-Winter 1987): 95-116.

Awcock, Frances. "Retrospective Conversion: Pipedream or Practicality?" *Australian Library Journal* 24, no. 1 (February 1985): 11-18.

Baber, Elizabeth A. "Planning for Retrospective Conversion at Rice University: Vendor and In-house Alternatives." In *Retrospective Conversion*, edited by Anne G. Adler and Elizabeth A. Baber. Ann Arbor: Pierian Press, 1984: 9-84.

Beaumont, Jane. *Retrospective Conversion: a Practical Guide for Libraries.* Westport, CT: Meckler, 1989.

Boss, Richard W. *Issues in Retrospective Conversion: Reproduced from a Report to McGill University.* (Presented as a part of the Proceedings of the CLASS Seminar on "Options in Retrospective Conversion."] San Jose: California Library Authority for Systems and Services, 1985.

Boss, Richard W. "Retrospective Conversion: Investing in the Future." *Wilson Library Bulletin* 59, no. 3 (Nov. 1984): 173-178, 238.

Bridge, Frank R. *Data Conversion: a Fundamental Step toward Library Automation: Participant Workbook.* [Text used for a workshop presented by the Library Development Division, Texas State Library.] Austin: Texas State Library, 1988.

Brown, Doris, R. "Retrocon for LCS in Illinois Academic Libraries." *Information Technology and Libraries* 3, no. 3 (Sept. 1984): 274-282.

Brown, Georgia L. "AACR2: OCLC's Implementation and Database Conversion." *Journal of Library Automation* 14 (Sept. 1981): 161-173.

Bruce, Jim. "An On-line Public-Access Catalogue: From Design through Retrospective Cataloguing." *School Libraries in Canada* 8 (Summer 1988): 48-55.

Burger, Robert H. "Conversion of Catalog Records to Machine-Readable Form: Major Projects, Continuing Problems, and Future Prospects." *Cataloging & Classification Quarterly* 3, no. 1 (Fall 1982): 27-40.

Carter, Ruth C. and Scott Bruntjen. *Data Conversion.* White Plains, NY: Knowledge Industry Publications, 1983.

Clayton, Peter. "Cost-Effective Retrospective Conversion of Monographs: a Selective Approach." *Cataloguing Australia* 14, no. 1 (March 1988): 15-19.

Collins, Gayle. "From Catalog to Database: Preliminary Steps." *School Library Journal* 31, no. 7 (March 1985): 123.

Collins, Jane D. "Planning for Retrospective Conversion." *Art Documentation* 1:3-4 (Summer 1982): 92-94.

Crawford, J. C. and others. "Database Creation and Management Glasgow College." *Program* 24: 33-43.

Cummings, G. "The Advocates Library: Online to 300 Years of History." *Library Association Record* 91 (March 1989): 153-154.

"Data Migration: We Have Met the Enemy and He/She/It Is Us." Papers presented at the annual conference of the California Library Association, San Diego, 1990. N. Hollywood, CA: Professional Programs, Inc. Cassette tape.

Drabenstott, Jon, ed. "Retrospective Conversion: Issues and Perspectives, a Forum." *Library Hi Tech* 4, no. 2 (Summer 1986): 105-120.

Enssle, Halcyon R. and Lou E. Anderson. "Conversion of Batch Records for Use in an Online System." *Information Technology and Libraries* 8, no. 3 (Sept. 1983): 317-325.

Epstein, Susan Baerg. "Converting Bibliographic Records for Automation: Some Options." *Library Journal* 108, no. 5 (March 1, 1983): 474-476.

Epstein, Susan Baerg. "Retrospective Conversion Revisited." Parts 1-3. *Library Journal* 115, no. 9 (May 15, 1990): 56-57; 115, no. 10 (June 1, 1990): 94-95, 98; 115, no. 12 (July 1, 1990): 66-69.

Finn, Maureen D. "How to Prepare for Retrospective Conversion." *Bulletin of the American Society for Information Science* 13, no. 4 (April/May 1987): 23-24.

Finn, Maureen D. "Retrospective Conversion, or 'How to Get Ready for Your Automated Future.'" *OCLC Newsletter* 166 (Jan. 1987): 9.

Foster, Constance L. "For Those Yet to be Converted: Suggestions for Libraries that are Still Using the Card Catalog." *Technicalities* 5, no. 8 (August 1985): 13-14.

Garland, Catherine. "PREMARC: Retrospective Conversion at the Library of Congress." *Fontes Artis musicae* 34 (April-Sept. 1987): 132-138.

Graves, Howard E. and Barbara Kolb. "Going Online: the End of the Line?" *Technicalities* 10, no. 9 (Sept. 1990): 12-14.

Gregor, Dorothy, ed. *Retrospective Conversion: Report of a Meeting Sponsored by the Council on Library Resources, July 16-18, 1984, Wayzata, Minnesota.* Washington: CLR, 1984.

"Guidelines for a Program for Coordinated Retrospective Conversion of Bibliographic Records for Monographs in U.S. and Canadian Libraries. Project Coordinator: Jutta Reed-Scott." Washington: Association of Research Libraries, 1985. Photocopy.

Hall, Sylvia Dunn. "High School Library Database: An Examination of Bibliographic Data Elements." Ph.D. diss., University of Pittsburgh, 1985.

Hirshon, Arnold. "The Emperor's New Bibliographic Clothes." *RTSD Newsletter* 10, no. 3 (1985): 28-30.

Hoadley, Irene B. and Leila Payne. "Toward Tomorrow: a Retrospective Conversion Project." *Journal of Academic Librarianship* 9(1983): 138-41.

Huggins, Annelle. "Retrospective Catalog Conversion: One Experience." *Tennessee Librarian* 35, no. 1 (Winter 1983): 29-33.

Information Systems Consultants Inc. *Retrospective Conversion for the Libraries of McGill University.* Montreal: McGill University, Libraries/ Systems Office, 1984.

Jacobs, Gijs J. M. "Retrospective Conversion. How many . . .?" *IFLA Journal* 16, no. 1 (Feb. 1990): 37-40.

Jackson, Kathleen L. "Rice University Speeds up its Conversion Project [including] Revised Rice University Specifications." In *Retrospective Conversion,* edited by Anne G. Adler and Elizabeth A. Baber. Ann Arbor: Pierian Press, 1984: 85-121.

Janakiev, Elisabeth and William Garrison. "Retrospective Conversion of Authority Records." In *Retrospective Conversion,* edited by Anne G. Adler and Elizabeth A. Baber. Ann Arbor: Pierian Press, 1984: 303-309.

John, Nancy. "Preparing for Online Access: Retrospective Conversion." *Illinois Libraries* 62, no. 7 (Sept. 1980): 619.

John, Patricia L. "Retrospective Conversion at the National Agricultural Library." In *Retrospective Conversion*, edited by Anne G. Adler and Elizabeth A. Baber. Ann Arbor: Pierian Press, 1984: 207-211.

Johnson, Carolyn A. "Retrospective Conversion of Three Library Collections." *Information Technology and Libraries* 1, no. 2 (June 1982): 133-139.

Jones, C. L. "Issues in Retrospective Conversion: Nine Recommendations for a Coordinated Program to Produce and Share Machine-Readable Bibliographic Records Nationally." *College and Research Libraries News* 10 (Nov. 1984): 528-532.

Kallenbach, S. F. "Retrospective Conversion." In *Proceedings of the First National Conference of the Library and Information Association, Sept. 17-21, 1983*. Chicago: American Library Association, 1983: 64-70.

Kepple, Robert J. "Retrospective Conversion." Paper presented at the 38th annual conference of the American Theological Library Association, Holland, Michigan, 1984. Cassette tape.

Krieger, Michael T. "Retrospective Conversion at a Two-Year College." *Information Technology and Libraries* 1, no. 1 (March 1982): 41-44.

Kroll, Carol. "Preparing the Collection for Retrospective Conversion." *School Library Media Quarterly* 18 (Winter 1990): 82-83.

Lambrecht, Jay H. "Reviving a Retrospective Conversion Project: Strategies to Complete the Task." *College and Research Libraries* 51, no. 1 (January 1990): 27-32.

LIBER Library Automation Group. "Guidelines for Retrospective Projects." *IFLA Journal* 16, no. 1 (Feb. 1990): 32-36.

Library of Congress, MARC Editorial Division. *MARC Conversion Manual–Authorities (Series): Content Designation Conventions and Online Procedures*. 2nd ed. Washington: Library of Congress, 1985.

Markuson, Barbara. *Plan for a North American Program for Coordinated Retrospective Conversion*. Washington: Association of Research Libraries, 1985.

McPherson, Dorothy S., Karen E. Coyle, and Teresa L. Montgomery. "Building a Merged Bibliographic Database: The University of California Experience." *Information Technology and Libraries* 1, no. 4 (Dec. 1982): 371-380.

Miller, Ruby E. "CORAL Conversion and Resource Enhancement Project." In *Retrospective Conversion*, edited by Anne G. Adler and Elizabeth A. Baber. Ann Arbor: Pierian Press, 1984: 201-206.

Murphy, Catherine. "Questions to Guide Retrospective Conversion Choices for School Library Media Centers." *School Library Media Quarterly* 18 (Winter 1990): 79-81.

OCLC, Inc. "Retrospective Conversion: Guidelines for Libraries." *Information Reports and Bibliographies* 17, no. 5 (1988): 21-24.

OCLC, Inc. *Guidelines for Libraries*. Dublin, OH: Online Computer Library Center, Inc., 1989.

Potter, William Gray. "Plans for an On-Line Catalog at the University of Illinois." *Resource Sharing & Library Networks* 1, no. 1 (Fall 1981): 53-63.

Purnell, Kathleen M. "Productivity in a Large-Scale Retrospective Conversion Project." In *Productivity in the Information Age: Proceedings of the 46th ASIS Annual Meeting 1983*. Washington, DC, October 2-6,1983. White Plains, NY: Knowledge Industry Publications, 1983:177-179.

Ra, Marsha H. *Retrospective Conversion in the RETRO Region*. Brooklyn, NY: METRO, 1986.

Racine, Drew. "Retrospective Conversion: a Challenge (Still) Facing Academic Libraries." *Show-Me Libraries* 36, no. 1-2 (Oct.-Nov. 1984): 39-43.

Ralls, Marion C. "The Evolution of a Retroconversion." *Vine* 57 (March 1985): 31-38.

Ramage, Pat. *Retrospective Conversion Manual: University Library Recon Project*. ERIC report: 265 880. Mobile, AL: University of South Alabama, 1985. Microfiche.

Rearden, Phyllis and John A. Whisler. "Retrospective Conversion at Eastern Illinois University." *Illinois Libraries* 65 (May 1983): 343-346.

Reed-Scott, Jutta. *Issues in Retrospective Conversion: Report of a Study Conducted for Council on Library Resources*. Washington: Council on Library Resources, 1984.

Reed-Scott, Jutta. *Plan for a North American Program for Coordinated Retrospective Conversion: Report of a Study Conducted for the Association of Research Libraries Committee on Bibliographic Control*. Washington: Association of Research Libraries, 1985.

Reed-Scott, Jutta. "Retrospective Conversion: an Update." *American Libraries* 16, no. 10 (Nov. 1985): 694-698.

Reed-Scott, Jutta. "Some Pointers on Retrospective Conversion." *Library Systems Newsletter* 3 (March 1983): 18-23.

Research Library Resources Access Project Final Report: a Retrospective Conversion Project Supported by a Grant under Title II C of the Higher Education Act. ERIC report: 217 843. Albany, NY: New York State Library, Cultural Education Center, 1982. Microfiche.

Retrospective Conversion. (SPEC Kit 130). Washington: Association of Research Libraries, Office of Management Studies, 1987.

Retrospective Conversion at Seven New England Libraries. Newton Upper Falls, MA: NELINET, 1984.

Ryans, Cynthia C. and Margaret F. Soule. "Preparations for Retrospective Conversion: an Empirical Study." *Catholic Library World* 55 (Dec. 1983): 221-223.

Schottlaender, Brian. "Retrospective Conversion and Special Cataloging Projects at UCLA." *DLA Bulletin* 8, no. 2 (Summer 1988): 16-17.

Settler, Leo H. "Retrospective Conversion: Getting Started." *Journal of Library Automation* 5, no. 1 (Spring 1984): 7-9.

Shaw, David. "A Computer-Based Catalogue of Books in Canterbury Cathedral Library." *Program* 18:3 (July 1984): 231-239.

Shurman, R. L. "Retrospective Conversion: The DuPage Library System Experience." *Illinois Libraries* 65 (May 1983): 337-339.

Skapura, Robert. "A Primer on Automating the Card Catalog." *School Library Media Quarterly* 18 (Winter 1990): 75-78.

Valentine, Phyllis A. and David R. McDonald. "Retrospective Conversion: a Question of Time, Standards, and Purpose." *Information Technology and Libraries* 5, no. 2 (June 1986): 112-120.

Vratny-Watts, Janet and Edward J. Valauskas. "Prospective Conversion: Data Transfer between Fossil and New Microcomputer Technologies in Libraries." *Information Technology and Libraries* 8, no. 1 (March 1989): 34-41.

Watkins, Deanne. "Special Reports: Record Conversion at Oregon State." *Wilson Library Bulletin* 60, no. 4 (Dec. 1985): 31-33.

Weber, Christine A. *Retrospective Conversion Manual.* Rochester, NY: University of Rochester Library, 1984.

Wells, Kathleen. "Retrospective Conversion: Through the Looking Glass." *RTSD Newsletter* 12, no. 1 (Winter 1987): 10-11.

Williams, Shirley. "How Important Is Retrospective Conversion?" *Arkansas Library* 46 (June 1989): 19-22.

Winter, Frank. "Conversion of a Non-MARC Database to MARC." *Information Technology and Libraries* 8, no. 4 (Dec. 1989): 442-451.

"Workshop on Retrospective Conversion." Presentations at the annual meeting of the American Association of Law Libraries, Chicago, 1987. Glendale, CA: Duplicated by Mobiltape Co. Cassette tape.

SAMPLING

DiCarlo, Michael A. and Margaret W. Maxfield. "Sequential Analysis as a Sampling Test for Inventory Need [Before Incurring the Cost of Retrospective Conversion.]" *Journal of Academic Librarianship* 13, no 6. (January 1988): 345-348.

Dougherty, Richard M. and Fred J. Heinritz. "Sampling." In *Scientific Management of Library Operations.* 2nd ed. Metuchen, NJ: The Scarecrow Press, 1982: 211-233.

Kawamoto, Chizuko. "File Analysis for Retrospective Conversion: the Case of the California State Library, Law Library." *Law Library Journal* 79 (summer 1987): 455-467.

STANDARDS AND QUALITY CONTROL

Chu, C. M. and others. "The Case of Tweddie-dee and Twedde-dum: Authority Control in a Retrospective Database." [Paper presented at the annual meeting of the Canadian Association for Information Science, June 25, 1986] *Canadian Journal of Information Science* 12, no. 1(1987): 35-37.

Crismond, Linda F. "Quality Issues in Retrospective Conversion Projects." *Library Resources & Technical Services* 25, no. 1 (Jan.-Mar. 1981): 48-55.

Fox, Steven J. "A Comparison of the Quality of Work Done by Catalog Technicians and Professional Catalogers in a Retrospective Conversion Project at the Salt Lake City Genealogy Library." M.L.S. research paper, Brigham Young University, 1984.

"Guidelines Proposed for Retrospective Conversion of Bibliographic Records of Monographs." *Library of Congress Information Bulletin* 44, no. 12 (March 25, 1985): 59-60.

Juneja, Derry C. "Quality Control in Data Conversion." *Library Resources & Technical Services* 31, no. 2 (April/June 1987): 148-158.

Knutson, G. S. A. "Comparison of Online and Card Catalog Accuracy." *Library Resources & Technical Services* 34, no. 1 (January 1990): 24-35.

Miller, Dan. "Authority Control in the Retrospective Conversion Process." *Information Technology and Libraries* 3, no. 3 (Sept. 1984): 286-292.

OCLC, Inc. "Transcription of Retrospective Copy." In *Online Systems: Bibliographic Input Standards.* 3rd ed. Dublin, OH: OCLC, 1985: 7-16.

RLG. *Approved Retrospective Conversion Projects: Procedural Guidelines for Cataloging.* RLG Document Code: 82-112. [Stanford, CA:] The Research Libraries Group, 1982.

Sule, Gisela. "Bibliographic Standards for Retrospective Conversion." *IFLA Journal* 16. no. 1 (Feb. 1990): 58-63.

COST STUDIES AND GRANT APPLICATIONS

Co, Francisca K. "An Investigation into the Economics of Retrospective Conversion Using a CD-ROM System." Specialist certificate, University of Wisconsin-Madison, 1988.

Co, Francisca K. "Retrospective Conversion on CD-ROM: a Cost Analysis [at Memphis State University Libraries.] *CD-ROM Librarian* 5, no. 1 (Jan. 1990): 11-20.

Johns, Cecily. "Everything You Always Wanted to Know about Getting a Title II-C Grant." *Technicalities* 3, no. 12 (1983): 8-9,16.

Peters, Stephen H. and Douglas J. Butler. "Cost Models for Retrospective Conversion Alternatives." *Library Resources & Technical Services* 28, no. 2 (Apr.-June 1984): 149-151.

Ra, Marsha H. "The Need for Costing in a Cooperative Retrospective Conversion Project [METRO Region]." *Technical Services Quarterly* 4, no. 4 (Summer 1987): 39-48.

OPTIONS, VENDORS, AND PRODUCTS

Bazillion, Richard J. and Susan Scott. "Ocelot Unleashed." *Canadian Library Journal* 42:155-158.

Beaumont, Jane. "Retrospective Conversion on a Micro: Options for Libraries." *Library Software Review* 5, no. 4 (July/Aug. 1986): 213-218.

Beaumont, Jane. "Retrospective Conversion on a Mirco [i.e., Micro]: Options." Presentation at SCIL Software/Computer Products Conference and Exposition, Peachtree Center, GA, 1986. Brooklyn, NY: Conference Copy, Inc. Cassette tape.

Bibi, Abd M. "CD-ROM for Retrospective Conversion: Selection of a Source Database." [Paper presented at CIL Conference 1989] *Library Software Review* 8 (July/Aug. 1989): 207.

Bibi, Abd M. "CD-ROM for Retrospective Conversion: the BRAZNET Experience[Brazoria County, Texas, Library Consortium]" *CD-ROM Library* 5 (Jan. 1990): 21-25.

Bibi, Abd M. "CD-ROM for Retrospective Conversion: the BRAZNET Experience [Brazoria County, Texas, Library Consortium]" *Library Software Review* 8 (Nov./Dec. 1989): 322-326.

Bocher, Robert. "MITINET/Retro in Wisconsin Libraries." *Information Technology and Libraries* 3, no. 3 (Sept. 1984): 267-274.

Chiang, Belinda. *Retrospective Conversion Through Carrollton Press: Manual of Procedures for Colgate University Libraries.* Hamilton, NY: Colgate University Libraries, 1984.

Clements, D. W. G. "Conversion of the General Catalogue of Printed Books to Machine-Readable Form [using OCR]" *Journal of Librarianship* 15:3 (July 1982): 206-213.

Cornell, E. Greek. "Computers and Libraries [using the Thesaurus Linguae Graecae CD-ROM]" *Library Review* 38, no. 5 (1989): 7-13.

Davidson, Josephine F. *The OCLC Retrospective Conversion Project of the L. E. Phillips Memorial Public Library: a Manual of Procedures.* Eau Claire, WI: The Library, 1982.

Desmarais, Norman. "BiblioFile for Retrospective Conversion." *Small Computers in Libraries* 5, no. 11 (Dec. 1985): 24-28.

Douglas, Nancy E. "Retrospective Conversion Using OCLC at Texas A & M University Library." In *Retrospective Conversion*, edited by Anne G. Adler and Elizabeth A. Baber. Ann Arbor: Pierian Press, 1984:1-7.

Douglas, Nancy E. "REMARC Retrospective Conversion: What, Why, and How." *Technical Service Quarterly* 2, no. 3/4 (Summer 1985): 11-16.

Drake, Virginia and Mary Paige Smith. "Retrospective Conversion with REMARC at Johns Hopkins University." *Information Technology and Libraries* 3, no. 3 (Sept. 1984): 282-286.

Epstein, Hank J. "MITINET/Retro: Retrospective Conversion on an Apple," *Information Technology and Libraries* 2, no. 2 (June 1983): 166-173.

Epstein, Hank J. "MITINET/Retro: Retrospective Conversion on an Apple." In *Retrospective Conversion*, edited by Anne G. Adler and Elizabeth A. Baber, 221-234. Ann Arbor: Pierian Press, 1984.

Ferrell, Mary Sue, and Carol A. Parkhurst. "Using LaserQuest for Retrospective Conversion of MARC Records." *Optical Information Systems* 7 (Nov./Dec. 1987): 396-400.

Final Report on Retrospective Conversion Project, State Library of Ohio [using OCLC] Dublin, OH: OCLC, User Services Division, 1981.

Hanson, Heidi and Greg Pronevitz. "Planning for Retrospective Conversion: a Simulation of the OCLC TAPECON Service." *Information Technology and Libraries* 8, no. 3 (Sept. 1989): 284-294.

Herrmann, Daphne. *The Batch Retrospective Conversion Program* [using RLIN] Stanford, CA: Research Libraries Group, 1988.

Hooten, P. A. A. "Preliminary Analysis of CAT CD450 for Retrospective Conversion for the Mid-Sized Research Library." *OCLC Micro* 6 (Feb. 1990): 18-20.

Jacso, Peter. "BiblioFile for Serials Cataloging." *Serials Librarian* 18, no. 1-2 (1990): 47-80.

Jacso, Peter. "CD-CATSS: UTLAS' Serial Compact Disk Database, a Review and Critique." *Serial Review* 15, no. 4 (1989): 7-18.

Lager, M. "SuperKey and the OCLC MicroCON Service." *OCLC Micro* 5 (April 1989): 21.

Latham, Joyce M. "LaserQuest: the General Research Corporation's CD-ROM Catalog." *Library Software Review* 8, no. 4 (July/Aug. 1989): 201-203.

Lisowski, Andrew and Judith Sessions. "Selecting a Retrospective Conversion Vendor." *Library Hi Tech* 1, no. 4 (Spring 1984): 65-68.

Lisowski, Andrew. "Vendor-Based Retrospective Conversion at George Washington University." In *Retrospective Conversion*, edited by Anne G. Adler and Elizabeth A. Baber. Ann Arbor: Pierian Press, 1984: 213-219.

MacMillan, Gary D. "UTLAS Discon: REMARC/MARC on CD-ROM in Hawaii." *CD-ROM Librarian* 2, no. 5 (Sept./Oct. 1987): 12-15.

McQueen, Judy and Boss, Richard. "Sources of Machine-Readable Cataloging and Retrospective Conversion." *Library Technology Reports* 21, no. 6 (Nov.-Dec. 1985): 597-732.

OCLC Retrospective Conversion Services. Dublin, OH: OCLC, 1985.

Pitkin, Gary M. "Conversion using OCR." In *Retrospective Conversion*, edited by Anne G. Adler and Elizabeth A. Baber. Ann Arbor: Pierian Press, 1984: 123-163.

Pohnl, Donald Robert. "Retrospective Conversion Using Microcomputers at the Park Falls Public Library: a Case Study." M.A. Seminar paper, University of Wisconsin-Oshkosh. 1985.

"Recon and REMARC at Edinburgh University Library." *Vine* 49 (August 1983): 13-18.

Ricker, Karina. "A Geac Library's Experience with MicroCON." *RTSD Newsletter* 12, no. 4 (Fall 1987): 44-46.

Russman, P. "Data Entry Planning for Retrospective Conversion [using MicroCON]" *College and Research Libraries News* 5 (May 1990): 456-460.

Saunders, Laverna M. "CD-ROM as a Cataloging Tool" [experience of Nevada academic and public libraries with General Research Corporation's LaserQuest] *Technical Services Quarterly* 6, no. 1(1988): 45-59.

Select MARC Retrospective Conversion: Here's How. Washington: Library of Congress, Cataloging Distribution Service, 1989.

Severtson, Susan. "REMARC: a Retrospective Conversion Project." *Program* 17, no. 4 (Oct. 1983): 224-232.

Shumaker, Lois E. "COM Catalog–the OCR Route." In *Retrospective Conversion*, edited by Anne G. Adler and Elizabeth A. Baber. Ann Arbor: Pierian Press, 1984:165-188.

"Spanish National Library Contract to Saztec." *Library Association Record* 91 (Dec. 1989): 695.

Velardi, Marie and James Lofferty. "MARC and INMAGIC: Tools for Developing an In-House Catalog; Retrospective Conversion is Achieved with INMAGIC." *Computers in Libraries* 10 (Dec. 1990): 14-18.

Woodburn, David M. and Gerald Buchanan. "Automation in Mississippi Public Libraries [using Auto-Graphics]" In *Retrospective Conversion*, edited by Anne G. Adler and Elizabeth A, Baber. Ann Arbor: Pierian Press, 1984:189-200.

SPECIAL ASPECTS OF RECON: TECHNICAL AND PROBLEM SOLVING

Caplan, Priscilla. "Retrospective Duplicate Resolution for the Harvard Distributable Union Catalog" *Information Technology and Libraries* 1, no. 2 (June 1982): 142-143.

Card, Sandra. "Problems and Solutions in a Retrospective Serials Conversion Project." In *Retrospective Conversion*, edited by Anne G. Adler and Elizabeth A. Baber. Ann Arbor: Pierian Press, 1984: 235-245.

Coyle, Karen. "Record Matching: a Discussion." *Information Technology and Libraries* 4, no. 1 (March 1985): 57-59.

Epstein, Susan Baerg. "Converting Records for Automation at the Copy Level." *Library Journal* 108, no. 7 (April 1, 1983): 642-643.

Hart, Amy "Operation Cleanup: the Problem Resolution Phase of a Retrospective Conversion Project." *Library Resources & Technical Services* 32, no. 4 (Oct. 1988): 378-386.

"Is There Life after Retrocon?" Papers presented at LITA/ALCTS Retrospective Conversion Interest Group during the annual conference of the American Library Association, June 23-28, 1990, at Chicago. Ballwin, MO: ACTS, 1990. Cassette tape.

Kruger, Kathleen Joyce. "MARC Tags and Retrospective Conversion: the Editing Process." *Information Technology and Libraries* 4, no. 1 (March 1985): 53-57.

Miller, Bruce. "Retroeff: a Retrospective Project Planning Spreadsheet." *Library Hi Tech* 6, no. 3 (1988): 40-42.

SPECIAL FORMATS/TYPES OF MATERIALS

Allen, Kimberly G. "Serial Conversion: One Supervisor's Account." *Technicalities* 3, no. 12 (Dec. 1983): 12-15.

American Association of Law Libraries. "Retrospective Conversion." Papers presented at the annual meeting of the Association, Washington, D.C. 1981. Glendale, CA: Mobiltape, 1981. Cassette tape.

American Association of Law Libraries. "Workshop on Retrospective Conversion." Recording of a workshop presented at the annual meeting of the Association in Chicago, 1987. Glendale, CA: Mobiltape, 1987. Cassette tape.

Banach, Patricia and Cynthia Spell. "Serial Conversion at the University of Massachusetts at Amherst." *Information Technology and Libraries* 7, no. 2 (June 1988): 124-130.

"Brandeis Hebraica Recon Project." *Technical Services Quarterly* 5, no. 2 (1987): 80-81.

Bratcher, Perry. "Music OCLC Recon: the Practical Approach." *Cataloging & Classification Quarterly* 8, no. 2 (1987/88): 41-48.

Broadway, Rita and Jane Qualls. "Retrospective Conversion of Periodicals: a Shoestring Experience." *Serials Librarian* 15, no. 1/2 (1988): 99-111.

Carter, Ruth C. "Cataloging Decisions on Pre-AACR2 Serial Records from a Union List Viewpoint." In *Union Lists: Issues and Answers.* Ann Arbor: Pierian Press, 1982: 77-80.

Chickering, S. and others. "A Conversion of Serials Records: OCLC LDR to VTLS USMARC format." *Information Technology and Libraries* 9, no. 3 (Sept. 1990): 263-271.

Copeland, Nora. "Retrospective Conversion of Serials: the RLIN Experience." *Serials Review* 14, no. 3 (1988): 23-28.

Dinkins, Rebecca Elsea. "Map Retro on a Shoestring." *Geography and Map Division Bulletin* [of the Special Library Association] 153 (Sept.1988): 3-10.

Dooley, Laura Gaston. *Retrospective Conversion of Music Collection: Project Manual: University of Tennessee, Knoxville Library, Cataloging Department, Retrospective Conversion Unit.* Knoxville, TN: The Library, 1984.

Ford, Margaret. "Retrospective Conversion of Music Material–streamlined." In *Retrospective Conversion,* edited by Anne G. Adler and Elizabeth A. Baber. Ann Arbor: Pierian Press, 1984: 293-302.

Green, Donald T. and Dean W. Corwin. "Retrospective Conversion of Music Materials." In *Retrospective Conversion,* edited by Anne G. Adler and Elizabeth A. Baber. Ann Arbor: Pierian Press, 1984: 247-291.

Katchen, Rosalie E. "Retrospective Conversion of Hebraica at Brandeis University." *Judaica Librarianship* 4, no. 1 (Fall 1987-Winter 1888): 20-22.

Kim, S. H. "Application of the USMARC Format for Holdings and Locations." *Serials Librarian* 16, no. 3-4(1989): 21-31.

Krumm, Carol R. "Conversion of Serial Holdings to On-Line Automated Library Control System at the Ohio State University Libraries." In *The Management of Serials Automation: Current Technology and Strategies for Future Planning,* edited by Peter Gellatly. New York: The Haworth Press, Inc. 1982: 83-94.

"Latin American Materials to be More Accessible." *College and Research Libraries News* 49, no. 11 (Dec. 1988): 743-744.

Lenzini, Rebecca T. and Eileen Koff. "Converting Serial Holdings to Machine-Readable Format, An Account of the University of Illinois-Urbana Experience."

In *The Management of Serials Automation: Current Technology and Strategies for Future Planning*, edited by Peter Gellatly. New York: The Haworth Press, Inc. 1982: 71-81.

Li, Weiming. "Retrospective Conversion of Serial Holdings to Machine Readable Form in the NSW Tafe Library Services." *Australia College Libraries* 6, no. 4 (Dec. 1988): 113-119.

Lowrey, James R. and Paul V. Hardiman. "Using a Text-Processing Language for Serial Record Conversion." *Information Technology and Libraries* 4, no. 4 (Dec. 1985): 356-358.

Lucker, Jay K. "Retrospective Conversion of Monographs in Technology." *IATUL Quarterly* [International Association of Technological University Libraries Quarterly] 1 (Sept. 1987): 216-224.

Lutz, Marilyn. "Retrospective Conversion of Government Documents." *LITA Newsletter* 10, no. 4 (Fall 1989): 13-14.

Mangan, Elizabeth Unger. *MARC Conversion Manual–Maps: Content Designation Conventions and Procedures for AACR2*. Washington: Library of Congress, Research Services, Geography and Map Division, 1984.

McKinley, Margaret M. "A Cooperative Serials Data Conversion Project in California." In *The Management of Serials Automation: Current Technology and Strategies for Future Planning*, edited by Peter Gellatly. New York: The Haworth Press, Inc. 1982: 95-106.

McKinley, Margaret M. "A Pragmatic Approach to Serials Data Conversion." *Serials Review* 7, no. 1 (Jan./Mar. 1981): 85-91.

Merritt, M. "University of Wyoming Library Conversion Project for English Fiction." *Action for Libraries* 10, no. 12(1984): 2-3.

Michaels, Carolyn Leopold and Kathryn S. Scott. "Daughters Plus: Retrospective Conversion at DAR." *Technicalities* 3, no. 3 (March 1983): 12-13.

Miller, Mary F. *Academic Law Libraries: the Status of Conversion to USMARC Format in OCLC, RLIN and WLN*. (American Association of Law Libraries Occasional paper, no. 6.) Chicago: American Association of Law Libraries, Publications Committee, 1987.

Millican, Rita. "Serials Conversion: LSU's Experience." *Serials Librarian* 9, no. 4 (Summer 1985): 45-51.

Nadeski, Karen. "The Restrospective [sic] Conversion of Microforms at Penn State." *Microform Review* 18 (Sept. 1989): 84-92.

"National Plan for Retrospective Conversion in Music." *Library of Congress Information Bulletin* 44, no. 30 (July 29, 1985): 205-206.

Pasternack, Howard. "Online Catalogs and the Retrospective Conversion of Special Collections." *Rare Books & Manuscripts Librarianship* 5, no. 2 (1990): 71-76.

Petersen, Karla D. "Planning for Serials Retrospective Conversion." *Serials Review* 10 (Fall 1984): 73-78.

Radke, Barbara and Teresa Montgomery. "CALLS ISSN Project." *Serials Review* 8, no. 2 (Summer 1982): 67.

"Retrospective Conversion of Government Documents" Recording of a program presented by the LITA/RTSD Retrospective Conversion Interest Group and the

Government Documents Round Table at the ALA Conference, Dallas, 1989. Ballwin, MO: ACTS. Cassette tape.

Retrospective Conversion of Music Materials: Report of a Meeting Sponsored by the Council of Library Resources, July 18-19, 1984, Wayzata, Minnesota. Washington: Council on Library Resources, Bibliographic Service Development Program, 1985.

Rose, Robert F. and S. J. Heron. "Disbanding a Special Collection: Methods and Labor Costs." *Collection Management* 11, no 1-2 (1989): 175-198.

Smith, Sharon and others. "Retrospective Conversion of Serials at the University of Houston: Midterm Report." *Serials Librarian* 9, no. 3 (Spring 1985): 63-68.

Stachacz, John C. "Small College Experience in Retrospective Conversion of Periodicals." *Information Technology and Libraries* 8, no. 4 (Dec. 1989): 422-430.

Steinhagen, E. N. "Monographic Series in Network Environment." *Serials Librarian* 16, no. 1-2 (1989): 65-74.

Tallman, K. D. and others. "Looseleaf Publications in Large Academic Libraries: the Looseleaf Recataloging Project at the University of Arizona." *Serials Librarian* 16, no. 3-4 (1989): 33-47.

Tucker, R. W. "Music Retrospective Conversion at the University of California at Berkeley." *Technical Services Quarterly* 7, no. 2 (1989): 13-28.

Tull, L. "Retrospective Conversion of Government Documents: the Marcive GPO Tape Clean-up Project." *Technicalities* 9 (Aug. 1989): 4-7.

Urbanski, Verna. "Retrospective Conversion of Audiovisual Materials." *RTSD Newsletter* 13, no. 6 (1988): 60-63.

Van Avery, A. R. "Recat vs. Recon of Serials: a Problem for Shared Cataloging." *Cataloging & Classification Quarterly* 10, no. 4(1990): 51-68.

Vick, Nancy. "Analyzing Atlases." *Information Bulletin of the Western Association of Map Libraries* 19, no. 1 (Nov. 1987): 30-32.

Weinberg, Bella Hass. "Retrospective Conversion of Hebraica Catalog Records: Options, Issues, and Visions." *Judaica Librarianship* 4, no. 1 (Fall 1987-Winter 1988): 17-20.

Wood, Susan. *Retrospective Conversion Procedure Manual for the Health Science Library.* Chapel Hill, NC: University of North Carolina at Chapel Hill, 1984. Typescript.

Wursten, Richard B. and James A. Chervinko. "Music Goes On-Line: Retrospective Conversion of Card Catalog Records for Music Scores at Morris Library (SIU-C)." *Illinois Libraries* 65 (May 1983): 346-348.

RECON IN AN INTERNATIONAL CONTEXT

Barry, Randall K. "Retrospective Conversion 'a la francaise' [joint conversion project of the American Library in Paris and the American University of Paris Library]" In *The Bowker Annual Library and Book Trade Almanac, 1990-91.* 35th ed. New York: Bowker, 1990: 206-212.

Bryant, Philip and Beaudiquez, Marcelle, eds. "Special Issue on Retrospective Catalogue Conversion, Retrospective Cataloguing and Retrospective Bibliography." *IFLA Journal* 16, no. 1 (Feb. 1990): 27-143.

Bryhn, Per Morten. "Conversion of Serials in a Networking Context." *IFLA Journal* 16, no. 1 (Feb. 1990): 49-51.

Campos, F. M. and F. C. Ferreira. "Adopting UNIMARC as a National Format: the Portuguese Experience [with Serials Data at the National Library]" *International Cataloguing & Bibliographic Control* 19 (April 1990): 22-26.

Delsey, Tom. "Retrospective Conversion in a Bilingual Context." *IFLA Journal* 16, no. 1 (Feb. 1990): 44-48.

Haddad, Peter. "The Catalogs of the National Library of Australia: Past, Present and Future." *Cataloguing Australia* 14, no. 4 (Dec. 1988): 2-6.

Hakli, E. "Retrospective Conversion of Catalogues in Helsinki University Library." *International Cataloguing & Bibliographic Control* 19 (April 1990): 27-29.

Igumnova, Natalia Petrovna. "The Development of a Retrospective National Bibliography in a Multinational State: a Study of the Experience of the USSR." [Revised translation of a paper given at the IFLA general conference, Chicago, 1985.] *International Cataloguing & Bibliographic Control* 16 (Oct. 1987): 44-46.

Jeremiah, David "Automation in the Department of Printed Books at the National Library of Wales, pt. 2: Cataloguing, Retrospective Conversion Enquiry and Circulation." *Program* 25 (Jan. 1991): 19-35.

Law, Derek. "Networking and Issues of Retroconversion." *IFLA Journal* 16, no. 1 (Feb. 1990): 52-54.

Law, Derek. "The State of Retroconversion in the United Kingdom: a Review" [Paper commissioned by the Centre for Catalogue Research at the University of Bath for presentation to the LIBER Working Group on Library Automation] *Journal of Librarianship* 20 (April 1988): 81-91.

Retrospective Conversion and Sources of Bibliographic Record Supply: a Review of the Options. London, England: Library & Information Technology Centre, 1990.

Simmons, P. A. "Converting UNIMARC Records to CCF [Unesco's Common Communication Format]" *International Cataloguing & Bibliographic Control* 18 (July 1989): 42-45.

Tickner, J. *Retrospective Conversion of the ARRB Catalogue*. Vermont South, Victoria: Australian Road Research Board, 1987.

Willemsen, A. W. "Retrospective National Bibliography: Operational Projects and Possible Future Developments in the Netherlands." *International Cataloguing & Bibliographic Control* 18 (Jan. 1989): 5-8.

MISCELLANEOUS

Cabral, Maria Luisa. "Copyright on Bibliographic Records." *IFLA Journal* 16, no. 1 (Feb. 1990): 41-43.

McCartney, Elizabeth J. "The Impact of Adding Retrospective Conversion Holdings to OCLC on Interlibrary Loan Lending." *RQ* 28, no. 3 (Spring 1989): 327-333.

"Ownership of Machine-Readable Records: a Neglected Consideration in Retrospective Conversion." *Library Systems Newsletter* 4, no. 6 (June 1984): 43-46.

Rockman, Ilene. "Retrospective Conversion: Reference Librarians are Missing the Action." *Library Journal* 115, no. 7 (April 5, 1990): 42-44.

Weibel, Stuart. "MARC-Up Catalog Card Conversion Prototype Explores Partial Automation of Retrospective Conversion." *OCLC Newsletter* 176 (Nov./Dec. 1988): 6-8.

BIBLIOGRAPHY

"Retrospective Conversion." In *Automation in Libraries: a LITA Bibliography, 1978-1982.* Ann Arbor: Pierian Press, 1983: 85-86.

Hogan, Walter P. "Retrospective Conversion: an Annotated Bibliography." In *Library Hi Tech Bibliography*, vol. 1, edited by C. Edward Wall. Ann Arbor: Pierian Press, 1986:107-114.

Retrospective Conversion: Selected Bibliography. (Bibliography, no. 55.) Toronto: University of Toronto, Faculty of Library and Information Science Library, 1987.

Williams, Shirley. "Retrospective Conversion: a Search of the Literature." *Arkansas Library* 45 (June 1988): 6-12.

PREMARC–
A History and Status Report

Susan H. Vita

SUMMARY. The Library of Congress' PREMARC file, conversion of which was completed in 1987, comprises approximately 5 million records from the Library's pre-1968 shelflist. The Library has mounted a concerted effort to improve the quality of these records by a process of comparison with the Library's Official Catalog. The Library is contemplating conducting a market survey to ascertain whether there is interest in the community in having PREMARC records distributed.

In 1977-78, University Microfilms International, with Carrollton Press, filmed the Library of Congress shelflist, publishing a microfilm copy in 1979. That same year, Carrollton announced that it would issue a printed title index to its microform version of the LC shelflist. It proposed to do so by generating the index from MARC records and its microform copy of non-MARC shelflist records, which it would convert into machine-readable form. At the same time, Carrollton approached the Library to determine whether we would be interested in purchasing the resultant machine-readable version of the shelflist for our local use. This would give the Library machine access to the older (pre-1968) records in its collection.

After further investigation and discussions, it was agreed that Carrollton would key the data and provide the Library with computer tapes containing these records in a "raw" state, i.e., there would

Susan H. Vita is Coordinator of Whole Book Cataloging at the Library of Congress. Previously, she was Chief of the MARC Editorial Division at the Library.

be no coding to identify fields within the records. The Library would then process the tapes through its Format Recognition computer program. This program automatically assigned machine-readable coding to the records, thereby identifying for the computer what part of the data represents (for example) an author's name, the title of the book, the subject headings, etc. We knew that there would be problems that would need correction, but we reasoned that this would give us a start at automating the pre-1968 portion of the Library's catalog. One copy of the processed records on tape was sent to Carrollton, and another copy was added to the Library's database.

The Library agreed to purchase a copy of all records not already in our MARC file for $0.3705 per record. The file conversion was completed in the fall of 1987. The entire operation involved 4.7 million records and cost the Library approximately $1,900,000. Carrollton Press named its version, which it marketed to the public, REMARC. The Library calls its version PREMARC. It is important to make the distinction between the two because although they were initially identical, there has been no attempt to keep the two files in sync, and over the years they have diverged.

In 1976 Carrollton Press was bought by Thomson International, as was UTLAS, the Canadian bibliographic utility. REMARC was acquired by UTLAS, and UTLAS is the current owner of the REMARC database.

Although the agreement with Carrollton placed no limit on the Library's own use of these records, limitations were placed on its distribution of the records. No more than 15,000 titles per year can be distributed for a period of 25 years, but any records which LC adds to the PREMARC file are not subject to distribution limitations. As the contract currently stands, unless other arrangements are made with UTLAS, it will be 2005 before LC has unlimited distribution rights to PREMARC. However, the Library and UTLAS have had several cordial discussions about the status of the REMARC/PREMARC file and the distribution rights over the past few years. It is hoped that were we to find ourselves in a position to begin to distribute the PREMARC records, some mutually acceptable agreement could be reached between UTLAS and LC to allow such distribution.

SCOPE

So what exactly is in the PREMARC file? The "shelflist" included in the original project had three parts:

1. The main or general shelflist. From this PREMARC includes the approximately 4 million non-MARC records present in the shelflist at the time it was filmed in 1978-1979. These records include books and serials–the latter converted to the books format.
2. The atlas and map shelflists.
3. The music shelflist.

These three categories totalled about 4.2 million records.

The Library and Carrollton later agreed to a second contract which included three additional groups of records:

1. The unclassified law shelflist;
2. Non-MARC records added to the shelflist after it was filmed, i.e., between 1978 and 1983. These are principally JACKPHY (Japanese, Arabic, Chinese, Korean, Persian, Hebrew, and Yiddish) language materials, music, and sound recordings.
3. Filmstrips and motion pictures in LC's collections and cataloged between 1952-68.

Together, this group amounted to an estimated 500,000 records. The records from the second contract have no distribution limitations on them.

Data elements originally included in PREMARC records:

LC card number (010)
LC call number (050)
LC copy statement (051)
Main entry (1XX)
Uniform title (240)–not always input
Title (245)–generally keyed only through the first "full thought"; statements of responsibility not input
Edition (250)

Imprint (260)–only the first place and name keyed when multiple places and publishers present; printers and/or distributors not included

Collation (300)–only "p. and cm." input in some early records

Subject headings (6XX)

Added entries (7XX)

Series added entries (8XX)

Language codes (041)

Geographic area codes (043)

Despite the above, the PREMARC file was not complete. At least 80,000 records were not keyed because they were unreadable. Moreover, only the classified collections are included. An estimated 125,000 Priority 4 records, precursors to minimal level cataloging, done in the 1930's, 1940's, and 1950's, were not in the main shelflist and were not in PREMARC.

Most of the records in the PREMARC file were created according to pre-1949 cataloging rules. However, one will find versions of all standard rules used by LC up to 1979. There are even some records added under the second contract that are in AACR2 form. But the vast majority of PREMARC records are in pre-AACR2 form. (It was this variety in cataloging rules that created the high error rate resulting from Format Recognition in the PREMARC file.)

Data elements not included in PREMARC records:

Dewey decimal classification number (082)

Untraced series (490)

Notes (5XX)

ISBN (020)

ISSN (022)

Superintendent of Documents number (086)

Price (350)

THE VALUE OF PREMARC

The primary value of PREMARC is that it is part of the Library's catalog–it contains the records for at least seventy years of LC's cataloging (1898-1968). However, as noted above, errors exist in many of the original 4.7 million records because the records were processed through the Format Recognition program without human review of the product. In order for people to find what is contained therein–and to locate the item represented by the catalog records–we must correct the errors.

The Format Recognition program was designed for *books* records cataloged under pre-AACR2 rules and pre-ISBD conventions. The PREMARC file, as noted above, consists of records representing serials, maps, music, filmstrips, motion pictures and sound recordings, as well as books, and all are forced into the books format. Most of these items were cataloged before the implementation of AACR1. The accuracy of the Format Recognition coding was further hindered by data errors. For example, the absence of a period after the abbreviation for "born" in the heading "Hall, Caroline Arabella, b 1838." caused format recognition to tag it as a corporate body rather than a personal name.

The addition of the PREMARC records to the machine readable catalog, however, made the older records, from 1898 to 1968, available for machine searching, and placed these records under some bibliographic control in the machine environment. For example, if one were to do the following search of the MARC file: FIND S FRANCE REVOLUTION 1789, one would get 1,900 hits. However, if the records in the PREMARC file were added to the search, one would retrieve an additional 398 records. Likewise, the search: FIND P MARIE ANTOINETTE in the MARC file yields 125 hits; the same search in PREMARC yields an additional 407 hits.

So the value of PREMARC, in spite of its inconsistencies and problems, is that it is the first step in making these additional five million records from the Library's catalog available for research. The main problem lies in the knowledge that errors may prevent additional records treating the desired topic in the file, and the items themselves, from being found. That is what the PREMARC cleanup project will correct.

PREMARC CLEANUP STRATEGY TESTING

Although the last PREMARC records converted by Carrollton Press were added to the database in the Fall of 1987, it was April

1988 before any cleanup was possible–prior to that date no input/update system was available. We could search the file, but not correct it. (The PREMARC file was set up separately from the file for the post-1968 records and not all applications were available in both files.) Now we have the capability to correct the errors that have been bothering us for years. It will be a long process. We're talking about five million records, after all! But we have taken our first baby steps to completion of the cleanup of the file. The summer of 1988 was spent learning and testing the new system, designing and performing tests of various approaches to cleanup, and working on documentation.

We determined that the cleanup would be achieved by assigning the MARC Editorial staff to the task as the cataloging done in the cataloging divisions was being done more and more online, freeing MARC Editorial staff to work on other tasks. These were the logical people, since they were experienced in MARC coding and in converting old and new records to the machine readable format.

Early on it was determined that the modus operandi would be to systematically pass through the Library's Official Catalog, a manual card catalog which currently contains only non-MARC Records, searching each card in the database, comparing the card with the corresponding PREMARC record, and correcting the PREMARC record to match the Official Catalog card. If the card was not in the PREMARC file, it was to be added.

The tests involved determining what changes would be made, and to what parts of the record. The information we were seeking would aid us in determining the degree of difficulty of each level of cleanup, and, consequently, the potential costs of the cleanup and the length of time it would take to complete the task, given different levels of staffing.

Three types of activity were tested:

1. Checking the content designation of the existing records;
2. Checking the validity of the data which was in the records;
3. Adding to the data which was in the records.

In addition we tested various levels of correction, from only correcting the call number, through complete correction of every record so that each would match completely the version in the Official Catalog.

All decisions on the final format for PREMARC were made in consultation with LC's internal users, e.g., the Law Library, the Congressional Research Service, the General Reading Room, etc. The final decision was to:

1. review and correct the tags and indicators of each field and, when appropriate, expand the subfield coding to reflect current practice;

2. for the following fields, validate the data in the PREMARC record, add any corrections or changes made to the appropriate fields from the Official Catalog card, and fill out the data in incomplete fields;

> LC card number (010)
> LC call number (050)
> LC copy statement (051)
> Main entry (1XX)
> Uniform title (240)
> Title (245)
> Edition (250)
> Imprint (260)
> Collation (300)
> Contents notes (505)
> Subject headings (6XX)
> Added entries (7XX)
> Series added entries (8XX)

3. add a note to records for non-book materials specifically identifying the type of material in order to provide for the possibility of later transferring these records to the appropriate file.

4. provide for including highly desirable information for some materials in special categories, e.g., rare books, and serials.

5. add a record history field (985) to each record, indicating in subfield g (maintenance code), the level of cleanup and, as appropriate, changes to individual fields that are unrelated to the Official Catalog comparison.

6. review and correct the following fixed fields:

008/35-39	language code
008/06	date type
008/07-10	date 1
008/11-14	date 2
008/15-17	country of publication code
008/39	descriptive cataloging form

Missing records will be added to the file and PREMARC records which duplicate records in other bibliographic files will be deleted.

As a result of further analysis of the various bibliographic situations represented in the Official Catalog and the desire to distinguish the records input by LC from those input by Carrollton Press, the following fields were subsequently added:

533	reproduction note
590	local note to reflect microform replacements
040	cataloging source
042	authentication code

Also, a newly defined value for retrospective records was added for use in the encoding level and the fixed field indicating the form of item was added.

It should be noted that PREMARC records will NOT be upgraded to AACR2. Subject headings will generally reflect the 9th edition of LCSH. Authority headings may not be current. No non-Roman material will appear; records will only include data in the romanized form. In addition, Geographic Area Codes (GACs) will not be checked.

Projections have been made for timetables to completion of the project, based on various staffing levels. The results which surfaced showed that this is no minor undertaking. To do the job as specified above with a staff of 6 will take 107 years; with a staff of 20 it will take 32 years; with a staff of 30 it will take 21.4 years; and with a staff of 40 it will take 16 years!

PREMARC CLEANUP STATUS

In February 1989, a PREMARC Unit was established in the MARC Editorial Division. Since that time most of the staff have worked on various PREMARC projects or the "OCAT pass," the process of comparing the Official Catalog (OCAT) entry against the corresponding PREMARC record and making the necessary changes and additions. Work on the OCAT pass, however, has been fitful due to the conflicting demands of arrearage reduction projects. The Library is now focusing on reducing the volume of its unprocessed materials and the MARC Editorial staff has participated by serving on details to custodial divisions and working on special projects. Occasionally an arrearage reduction project involves the PREMARC file and the needs for PREMARC cleanup and arrearage reduction are both served. Current plans are for a staff of approximately 25 devoted to the PREMARC cleanup, possibly supplemented by work performed on contract.

Through November 1991 the following actions have been performed against the PREMARC file:

1. The deletion of 50,000 PREMARC records which duplicated records on other bibliographic files or were invalid.

2. The editing of 176,350 records to correct errors reported by the reference and cataloging staff members or to make proactive changes initiated by the MARC Editorial staff, including OCAT pass changes.

3. The addition of 138,000 records which were not included in the original Carrollton Press agreement or were overlooked. Some of these represent pamphlet collections, but the largest number (126,110 records) represent items which were given Priority 4 cataloging, a form of minimal level cataloging done from the 1930's to the 1950's.

Included in the cleanup activity above were changes made for the following purposes:

The correction of the content designation in records where it was so erroneous that the records lacked a call number field, even though the call number was present.

Supplying correct LC card numbers for records which Carrollton Press added to the file with pseudo numbers because the number on their photographic image was illegible or the original was a temporary card which lacked a card number.

The correction of typographical errors which interfered with retrieval of the headings for the United States (spelled Untied States!), Great Britain, Lenin, Chopin, Willa Cather (tagged as a uniform title), Albert Schweitzer, and Columbus. Other misspellings which were corrected were for the words: church, poems, school, republic, railroads, psalms, commission, committee, civilization, etc.

The correction of the content designation for records in which all the fields were mistagged, usually as notes.

The addition of preservation microfilm information to PRE-MARC records. The presence of this information in the PRE-MARC records facilitates location of the material by users and made it possible to discard the manual charge file which held this information.

Currently the MARC Editorial staff is adding to PREMARC the 80,000 records which were not converted by Carrollton Press because they were unreadable. The slips were returned to MARC Editorial, which conducted a search project in 1986 to obtain legible copy of the catalog entries. Through November 1991, about 2,000 records have been added.

An instruction manual for PREMARC cleanup is almost complete. Lacking are instructions for music, sound recordings, and audio-visual materials. The field-by-field conversion manual is complete but subject to constant revisions as new situations are encountered.

DISTRIBUTION

Distribution of the PREMARC file remains a problem with many unanswered questions–the biggest of which is, is there a market for these records? Five million records would be the equivalent of about 20 years of MARC tape subscriptions. Would anyone want to purchase the file?

1. Currently there is no software written to distribute PREMARC. It would be a simple task, but automation resources would have to be assigned to do it. Need for distribution of the records will have to be established in order for these automation resources to be reassigned.

2. Contractual limitations still might prohibit unlimited distribution until 2005.

3. Informal studies have shown that 65% of the PREMARC records reside on OCLC in some form. Presumably a similarly high percentage would be found on the RLIN database. And UTLAS has the complete file–although it does not currently reflect the changes that LC will be making. There is some question whether these utilities would want to load the PREMARC file onto their databases.

4. The need for these records externally is unknown. Although the PREMARC records are an essential part of LC's internal catalog, we do not know how useful they are to other libraries, given the fact that they will not be upgraded to AACR2 and beyond the ninth edition of LCSH. How useful will they be as time goes on? Have most libraries already completed retrospective conversion projects? Will those that have not finished find the speed at which PREMARC is cleaned up to be too slow to be helpful?

LC could conceivably distribute close to 820,000 records in the near future, including the 500,000 records without distribution limitations and the new records that we will be inputting, if the software were available. But is there a need to distribute the PREMARC records? The question is relevant, since the task of preparing to distribute the PREMARC file will divert automation resources from other priorities. The question was asked at ALA in 1990 before the LITA/ALCTS Retrospective Conversion Interest Group, which included an audience of approximately 200 technical services librarians interested in retrospective conversion. The audience response indicated that not enough libraries would be interested in the distribution to warrant LC's placing a high priority on this activity at this time. Given that response and the constraints mentioned above, plans to distribute PREMARC records have been placed on hold. However, the Cataloging Distribution Service is considering doing market research to verify the external need for PREMARC.

CONCLUSION

- The PREMARC File is part of LC's catalog and, consequently, is a valuable research tool which LC needs to clean up in order to gain the full benefit of access to the records contained in it.

- For the present, a limited number of staff will be assigned to continue this work while others work on cataloging current material and processing the uncontrolled arrearages.
- Cleanup will be time consuming. (The length of time will depend on the resources that can be devoted to the task. At current levels of staffing it will take more than 30 years to complete.)
- Contracts are being investigated for the purpose of supplementing the PREMARC work being done by LC staff, perhaps allowing us to complete the project sooner.
- Distribution of the PREMARC records does not appear to be a high priority of the library community at this time, so it is currently on hold.

CASE STUDIES

Retrospective Conversion
of a Medium-Sized Academic Library

Mary K. Bolin
Harley B. Wright

SUMMARY. Even a successful retrospective conversion project requires a great deal of time, money, staff and problem-solving. The University of Idaho Library is a medium-sized academic library and a member of WLN. This article describes the methods the library used to convert its collection, and examines the problems encountered with each method.

INTRODUCTION

Retrospective conversion (recon), the building of a MARC database from manual cataloging records, is one of the fundamental activities on the road to library automation. The literature emphasizes careful planning and consideration of the long-term implications of decisions which are made.[1] Even the most careful planning probably will not allow a library to avoid all problems, however,

Mary K. Bolin is Head, Cataloging Department and Harley B. Wright is Copy Cataloging Coordinator. Both are affiliated with the University of Idaho Library, Moscow, ID 83843.

and even the most well-organized project may be plagued by unforeseen difficulties. The University of Idaho (UI) Library accomplished its database conversion in a fairly short time and with a minimum of difficulties; nevertheless, there were problems, some of which we are still discovering. Moreover, recon is expensive, no matter what method is chosen, and while the benefits of having our holdings in MARC format are incalculable, the cost of conversion, in library staff time and vendor charges, was considerable.[2]

The UI library is a medium-sized academic library with nearly 2,000,000 total volumes, which has been a member of WLN (formerly the Western Library Network) since 1979. At the time the library joined WLN, we closed the card catalog but continued to maintain a paper shelflist. Until 1983 the library used WLN's Resource Directory, a microfiche version of the WLN database, as its public catalog. From 1983 until 1988, we produced a microfiche catalog of UI holdings only. The Cataloging Department now has four librarians and eleven paraprofessional staff. During the time of the recon project, we had 4.5-5.5 librarians and 14 FTE paraprofessionals. Cataloging is centralized, and we normally catalog 15-20,000 titles per year, including books, serials, scores, sound recordings, computer files, and some maps and government documents.

The UI library has converted virtually all of its holdings, has discarded its card catalog and relies on machine-readable records. The card catalog was disposed of in the fall of 1988, when nonserial recon was finished. At that time we stopped producing a COM catalog, and adopted WLN's LaserCat CD-ROM catalog as our public catalog. At least four years of hard work and considerable expense led to that very desirable step.

EARLY ATTEMPTS

At the UI library, we began retrospective conversion in the mid-1980s, taking a number of different approaches. The first recon technique we tried was WLN's WYLBUR text-editing system. Library staff input information for unconverted items into the WYLBUR system using WLN terminals, and WLN then created a magnetic tape which it ran against its database four times a year, looking for matching records. When a match was found, the library's call number was attached to the holdings records for that item. Once run, a tape could be held and run again. The cost was $.27 per hit. On the first pass, the hit rate was as high as 80% for parts of the general collections and 30% for our special collections. Each subsequent match found fewer and fewer records until we felt it was no longer worth trying again. This first step to recon was a logical and inexpensive approach, and from September 1980 until March 1986, we converted 119,202 records this way. At the height of this project, the entire library was involved. Volunteers from all departments signed up for one-hour time slots, and the terminals were busy from 8:00 a.m. to 6:00 p.m.

GRANT TO CONVERT REGIONAL MATERIAL

In 1985, an LSCA grant to convert the 5,400 titles in the library's Day-Northwest (Day-NW) collection (materials of regional interest) got us started on the systematic recon effort which would last for a number of years. The grant request was for $11,750, plus approximately $20,000 in local matching funds, making the entire amount for the project approximately $32,000. A temporary, high-level paraprofessional position was created to oversee the project. A library assistant who had worked in cataloging for several years was hired to fill that position. In addition, another temporary library assistant job was created specifically for the recon project, and one permanent library assistant position from cataloging was dedicated to the project. As much as eighty hours per week of "irregular help" (student and other hourly workers) were also devoted to recon. The recon project was housed in a small, separate office, on the same floor of the library as the Cataloging Department, but at a short distance from it. The office had its own WLN terminal, printer and high-quality photocopier.

CONTRACTING WITH SAZTEC

The library contracted with the Saztec Corporation of Eugene, Oregon to create MARC records for the 5,400 Day-Northwest items. As part of the planning stage, Saztec created a 35-page data conversion specification document giving specific instructions for tagging and keying the records.[3] UI library staff reviewed and responded to that document. When the conversion specifications and service agreement (which dealt with the schedule, price and quality of the project) were completed and signed, UI library recon staff began photocopying shelflist cards for unconverted monographic items. They searched the WLN database, finding matching records for 35% of the material. Holdings for these were attached via WYLBUR. Photocopies of the remainder were mailed to Saztec. Saztec staff in the Philippines created records which WLN loaded into a separate input file, to be edited and verified into the WLN database. After these records were converted, the library received more funding for recon and contracted with Saztec to convert more of the collection, and 8,000 more records were keyed and loaded. Several catalog librarians began to spend some time helping to verify these records. Although Saztec's work was timely and accurate, there were a number of problems with the records they created. The information was exactly as it appeared in the shelflist, so that name, subject and series headings had to be changed to AACR2 forms before the records entered the database. In addition, there were fill characters in some parts of the records which had to be removed. Moreover, since the records were converted by Saztec employees who were unfamiliar with the elements of a catalog record, and who were not necessarily native speakers of English, some information, especially from Library of Congress printed cards, was transcribed incorrectly. (For example, a cross reference from a Library of Congress (LC) printed card, e.g., "Full name: John Robert Martin Smith" might be erroneously transcribed and tagged as a note or an added entry. When information appeared on both sides of the hole in the bottom of the card, it was sometimes transcribed with a large space in the middle.)

In addition to the editing which had to be done to these records, there were a number of initial problems with loading the tapes into WLN's input file which caused delays. Some of these were problems with the data on the tapes. For example, one large group of records was input with the wrong library location; another group had the wrong encoding level for records with LC card numbers; and another the wrong country of publication code in the fixed field. One large group of records was entered using record identifier numbers (a unique access point) which had already been used and yet another group was created with an incorrect subfield "a" in the 984 (holdings) field. Saztec recreated all of those records except for the last group, and gave the library a reduced charge for the "trouble factor" involved in fixing the incorrect 984's. Despite the company's cooperative attitude, however, there were delays. Other problems were the result of WLN's tapeloading program. (Considerable work has since been done on that program to correct these.) For example, when records were loaded into WLN, those with LC card numbers always sorted first. This meant that UI recon staff could not review records in shelflist order. Further, subject headings and added entries on each record were rearranged into numerical tag order rather than the order they appeared in on the card. (This is probably not earthshaking, but catalogers have conventionally assigned subject headings and added entries in a sort of hierarchical order.)

COSTS OF THE SAZTEC PROJECT

Tape 1	test batch–Day-NW collection	$761.10
	501 records @ $1.52	
Tape 2	remainder of Day-NW collection	$3,325.66
	2338 records @ $1.42	
Tape 3	UI theses and dissertations	$3,069.59
	2442 records @ $1.26	
Freight	September-June	$370.09
Project development fee		$2,500.00
TOTAL		$10,026.44
WLN tapeload .05/record		$264.05
Saztec discount–"trouble factor" plus		($1,723.56)
keystroke/record decline cost		
(Saztec charged $1.00 per 1000 keystrokes, up to a certain number after which the cost declined)		
TOTAL		$8,566.93

Aside from the delays in loading the Saztec records into WLN's input file, the amount of authority work and other editing which had to be done to the records made this method too time-consuming and labor-intensive. UI recon staff found it very difficult to keep up with the work involved in verifying the records into the database. Moreover, it became very difficult to coordinate activities going on in six different locations: library staff in Moscow; WLN in Olympia, Washington; WLN's computer staff in Pullman, Washington; and Saztec staff in Eugene, Oregon, the Philippines and Dayton, Ohio. The library decided to contract with WLN to complete the conversion of its collection.

CONTRACTING WITH WLN

UI recon staff continued systematically going through the shelflist, searching WLN for matching records. All cards were photocopied, and searching was done from the photocopies. When a match was found, our holdings were attached to the record. Recon staff were able to attach holdings to about 1,500 database records each month, and prepare photocopies of 2,000 more records to send to WLN for tagging and inputting each month. WLN recon staff (part of the network's Cataloging/Inputting Service) created records from the photocopied cards and wrote the system-assigned control number on the photocopies. After WLN returned the photocopies to us, the last step was for UI recon staff to stamp "WLN" on the shelflist card for converted records and also to transcribe the control number onto the card.

Although WLN was not able to begin inputting until January of 1987, and although they did not always convert as many records per month as they had estimated, our holdings went from 247,000 in September of 1986 to 360,000 in September 1988. Since new cataloging adds about 15-20,000 holdings per year, the recon project converted approximately 40-50,000 records. UI recon staff finished sending photocopies of non-serial records to WLN in the Fall of 1987, but WLN did not finish inputting until the following Summer. Recon activity was reflected in our monthly WLN statistics–about 35,000 inquiries (up about 10,000), 3500 holdings attached (up about 2000) and 2000 records input (up about 1700) per month.

COST

While we feel that the effect of recon has been immeasurably beneficial, and while our project went smoothly for the most part, converting from paper to computerized records is always expensive.

The most expensive component of the project was staff. Two temporary library assistant positions were created, and 80 hours per week of "irregular help" were devoted to recon.

LAIII	$22,320.00	(library assistant salaries
LAI	$18,600.00	include 24% for benefits.)
Hourly workers	$21,340.80	
Total per year	$62,260.80	
Total for project	$186,782.40	

Our in-house recon activity added to our WLN charges. One terminal was devoted to recon, although other terminals were also used for the project. Searching the database before sending records to WLN created charges for inquiries and for attaching holdings to records found. WLN charged $2.85 per record for books and serials. That included inputting a record from the photocopy of the cataloging card, attaching holdings to that record, plus a charge for one inquiry per record. If our shelflist card had inadequate information, we would indicate that on the photocopy which went to WLN, and they would order a new card at a cost of $.50 per record plus $.08 for the card. We ordered a new card as infrequently as possible to keep costs down (see Appendix).

OTHER PROBLEMS

While the phase of the project done by WLN went remarkably smoothly for the most part, there were still a few difficulties. A major annoyance encountered at the beginning of the project was the library's earlier practice, before the card catalog was closed, of filing only the first card of a multiple card set in the shelflist, so that complete information was found only in the public catalog. Recon staff had to search the public catalog for incomplete card sets before those records could be sent to Saztec or WLN, since often the subject headings and other added entries were missing. The cost in staff time for reconstructing these entries was enormous and regrettable.

A more understandable problem was the clean-up which any recon project entails.[4] One approach we used was to have an experienced staff member go through the shelflist card by card, finding cards which were not stamped (and therefore had not been converted), as well as other snags and problems. These several last passes through the shelflist were dubbed "final recon" and "ultimate recon." Many of the problems encountered were serial vs. monograph problems, which were flagged and attended to during serial recon, which followed in 1988. Other problems were brought to us by staff in other departments. These were most often incorrect call numbers, holdings attached to the wrong record, etc. Each generation of catalogers likes to revile its forbears, and we are no exception: one barrier to converting our shelflist to machine-readable form was that the information on the cards was often inadequate or erroneous. We found that it was better not to go to the stacks and get the item to compare it to the cards, because most often the two bore little resemblance to each other. Our project was to convert the shelflist–such as it was, in some cases, not to recatalog the collection.

Two problems arose while recon was going on or after it was finished. First was the understandable impatience of some library staff, especially those in public services, to have the project finished. The considerable money going to recon was sometimes seen as a drain on the Library's budget, never flush at the best of times. In addition, the Cataloging Department was sometimes too optimistic about the project's timetable, giving people the impression that it would be finished sooner than was possible.

The second problem was keeping up the morale of the recon staff. The recon unit had a feeling of separateness, although they were part of the Cataloging Department. This separateness was sometimes healthy, because it fostered team spirit, and helped us reach our goal faster. However, since the unit was physically separated from the rest of Cataloging, it was harder to integrate recon staff into departmental procedures, workflow and communication. The fact that most of the recon staff were in temporary positions made these problems worse. After the project had been underway for a few months, recon staff began dividing their time between recon and other cataloging tasks, such as searching WLN for records for new books and attaching holdings. This had both good and bad results. While they had developed a lot of skill with bibliographic data, they had some difficulty distinguishing recon procedures and standards from those for processing new materials. For example, for the purposes of recon we allowed much more leeway in the date of publication when deciding whether a database record was a match than we do when processing new materials. It was sometimes hard for recon staff to keep these distinctions in mind.

Certain formats were more difficult to deal with than others. The MARC Maps Format was not available on WLN at the time we did conversion, so that that part of the collection could not be added to the database. When we got to the "M's" (music) in our shelflist, we found that it was harder to search the database for scores and sound recordings, since WLN has powerful keyword searching but no exact title search. (WLN has since improved its searching software in ways which would have alleviated some of these difficulties.) The often generic titles of scores and sound recordings made them hard to retrieve.[5] WLN occasionally had staffing problems–unfilled positions or lots of turnover, which made it hard at times to finish conversion, especially when particular expertise was required, as with music. There was sometimes a time-lag between the time we sent photocopies to WLN and they were able to convert the records. This meant that a certain percentage of those records would already be in the database by the time WLN staff were ready to input a record. This added to the cost of the project, since WLN charged more to attach holdings to an existing record than it would have cost us to do it in the library.

BENEFITS

There have been a number of desirable results from having the non-serial part of recon finished. First, was the most obvious–we could get rid of the card catalog and rely on WLN's CD-ROM LaserCat as our public catalog. While there are patrons who mourn the card catalog and are sickened by what they see as the waste of having discarded it, most patrons and staff welcome the flexibility of LaserCat. A second benefit is the addition of highly trained staff to the Cataloging Department. During the course of the project, we began to make fuller use of the skills they developed while doing retrospective conversion. Recon staff were responsible for a significant proportion of our copy and adaptive cataloging output, and also did many other tasks such as inputting original records. It might have been nice to have kept all of the positions which were created for recon when the project was over. As it happened, we kept only the Library Assistant III who supervised the project. This position has evolved into a Copy Cataloging Coordinator and original cataloger. The other temporary library assistant position is no longer in the Department, although the person who filled that position now occupies another, higher-level position in Cataloging. Likewise with the hourly staff: none of those hours remained in the Department, although most of the staff who filled those hours now have permanent positions in technical services.

CONCLUSION

A library contemplating recon can learn several things from the successes and failures of this project. These things may be obvious, but they bear repeating.

1. Set a realistic timetable. Some factors will be out of the library's control, even if recon is done entirely in-house.

2. Create "clean" records to start, rather than creating records which need editing or updating. WLN's recon service created records with all headings in their most up-to-date form. The price we paid for these records was worth it, since this will save us money when we load these records into a local system.

3. The clean-up phase is crucial to finishing recon, and therefore it should be systematic.

4. Only a very well-staffed library with a very small collection can afford to consider recon as an opportunity for wholesale recataloging.

NOTES

1. For an excellent, concise discussion of this see, Susan Baerg Epstein, "Retrospective Conversion Revisited, Part 1," *Library Journal* 115, no. 9 (May 15, 1990): 56-57 and Susan Baerg Epstein, "Retrospective Conversion Revisited, Part 2," *Library Journal* 115, no. 10 (June 1, 1990): 95-98. Another practical planning guide is Jane Beaumont and Joseph Cox, *Retrospective Conversion: a Practical Guide for Libraries*. Supplements to Computers in Libraries, no. 7. (Westport, Conn.: Meckler, 1989.)

2. Retrospective conversion costs are treated by Marsha Ra, "The Need for Costing in a Cooperative Retrospective Conversion Project," *Technical Services Quarterly* 4, no. 4 (Summer 1987): 39-48 and Marion T. Reid and K.L. Wells, "Retrospective Conversion through the Looking Glass, *RTSD Newsletter* 12 (1987): 10-11.

3. A thorough treatment of the problems of data conversion is Ruth C. Carter and Scott Bruntjen, *Data Conversion* (White Plains, N.Y.: Knowledge Industry Publications, 1983.) Other sources in this area include Richard W. Boss and Hal Espo, "Standards, Database Design & Retrospective Conversion," *Library Journal* 112, no. 16 (October 1, 1987): 54-8 and Derry C. Juneja, "Quality Control in Data Conversion," *Library Resources and Technical Services* 31, no. 2 (April/June 1987): 148-58.

4. This portion of recon is described by Amy Hart, "Operation Cleanup: the Problem Resolution Phase of a Retrospective Conversion Project," *Library Resources and Technical Services* 32, no. 3 (October 1988): 378-86.

5. For a detailed treatment of the problems encountered in music conversion see Ruth Tucker, "Music Retrospective Conversion at the University of California at Berkeley," *Technical Services Quarterly* 7, no. 2 (1989): 13-28.

APPENDIX

MONTH:	Jul/87	Aug/87	Sep/87	Oct/87	Nov/87	Dec/87
CATALOGING						
INQUIRIES	$2,291.22	$2,124.44	$3,359.78	$3,621.02	$2,843.71	$2,570.47
ATTACH HOLDINGS	$804.60	$423.00	$389.20	$312.80	$347.80	$419.40
RCP (ORDER CARDS)	$316.65	$261.90	$325.50	$231.90	$233.55	$266.55
INPUT NEW RECORDS	$73.50	$91.05	$0.94	$24.30	$47.85	$51.00
WLN RECON INPUT	$3,712.50	$5,906.00	$5,932.80	$5,912.80	$3,933.55	$4,818.30
WLN CONTRACT CATALOGING	$3,655.40	$2,485.15	$3,839.05	$1,575.05	$1,949.90	$852.20
CATALOG CARDS	$526.78	$441.68	$645.76	$455.68	$430.32	$405.12
TERMINAL MAINTENANCE	$240.00	$240.00	$280.00	$280.00	$280.00	$280.00
MODEM MAINTENANCE	$15.00	$15.00	$15.00	$15.00	$15.00	$15.00
TERMINAL CONNECT CHARGE	$960.00	$960.00	$1,120.00	$1,120.00	$1,120.00	$1,120.00
CATALOGING TOTAL	$12,595.65	$12,948.22	$15,908.03	$13,548.55	$11,201.68	$10,798.04

	Jan/88	Feb/88	Mar/88	Apr/88	May/88	Jun/88	FY TOTAL
INQUIRIES	$2,015.75	$2,338.41	$2,359.95	$2,246.95	$1,893.00	$1,889.15	$29,553.86
ATTACH HOLDINGS	$293.60	$334.40	$332.40	$347.20	$297.80	$413.20	$4,715.40
RCP (ORDER CARDS)	$254.70	$271.65	$268.95	$254.55	$281.25	$160.20	$3,127.35
INPUT NEW RECORDS	$73.65	$41.25	$145.05	$94.05	$39.00	$58.05	$739.69
WLN RECON INPUT	$5,599.15	$5,061.00	$5,716.60	$5,915.30	$6,070.35	$5,450.45	$64,028.80
WLN CONTRACT CATALOGING	$373.85	$17.85		$17.85			$14,766.30
CATALOG CARDS	$394.56	$481.53	$415.68	$397.92	$507.36	$247.60	$5,349.99
TERMINAL MAINTENANCE	$200.00	$200.00	$200.00	$200.00	$200.00	$200.00	$2,800.00
MODEM MAINTENANCE	$15.00						$105.00
TERMINAL CONNECT CHARGE	$800.00	$800.00	$800.00	$800.00	$800.00	$800.00	$11,200.00
CATALOGING TOTAL	$10,020.26	$9,546.09	$10,238.63	$10,273.82	$10,088.76	$9,218.65	$136,386.39

APPENDIX (continued)

MONTH:	Jul/88	Aug/88	Sep/88	Oct/88	Nov/88	Dec/88
CATALOGING						
INQUIRIES	$1,512.20	$1,437.95	$1,627.25	$1,618.25	$1,573.35	$2,005.90
ATTACH HOLDINGS	$338.50	$260.75	$250.75	$191.50	$207.50	$332.75
RCP (ORDER CARDS)	$176.40	$121.35	$135.45	$145.20	$121.50	$188.40
INPUT NEW RECORDS	$239.40	$74.25	$66.30	$166.35	$387.75	$138.30
WLN RECON INPUT	$4,348.00	$603.70	$2,016.75	$2,392.00	$10,709.05	$497.20
CATALOG CARDS	$262.08	$199.84	$211.68	$209.84	$173.68	$235.92
TERMINAL MAINTENANCE	$125.00	$125.00	$125.00	$125.00	$125.00	$125.00
TERMINAL CONNECT CHARGE	$925.00	$925.00	$925.00	$925.00	$925.00	$925.00
CATALOGING TOTAL	$7,926.58	$3,747.84	$5,358.18	$5,773.14	$14,222.83	$4,448.47

CATALOGING	Jan/89	Feb/89	Mar/89	Apr/89	May/89	Jun/89	FY TOTAL
INQUIRIES	$2,454.60	$2,360.10	$2,764.90	$2,929.05	$3,085.25	$2,833.50	$26,202.30
ATTACH HOLDINGS	$328.25	$324.25	$393.00	$376.75	$500.50	$490.25	$3,994.75
RCP (ORDER CARDS)	$150.15	$220.95	$195.15	$282.90	$339.60	$299.25	$2,376.30
INPUT NEW RECORDS	$44.70	$42.00	$53.40	$37.20	$47.90	$58.45	$1,356.00
WLN RECON INPUT	$194.08	$184.40	$282.30			$71.50	$21,104.90
CATALOG CARDS		$278.00	$255.76	$350.80	$421.44	$358.40	$3,151.52
TERMINAL MAINTENANCE	$125.00	$125.00	$125.00	$125.00	$125.00	$125.00	$1,500.00
TERMINAL CONNECT CHARGE	$925.00	$925.00	$925.00	$925.00	$925.00	$925.00	$11,100.00
CATALOGING TOTAL	$4,221.78	$4,459.70	$4,994.51	$5,026.70	$5,444.69	$5,161.35	$70,785.77

APPENDIX (continued)

MONTH:	Jul/89	Aug/89	Sep/89	Oct/89	Nov/89	Dec/89
CATALOGING						
INQUIRIES	$2,024.30	$2,689.73	$2,779.60	$3,024.85	$2,879.40	$2,787.00
ATTACH HOLDINGS	$309.30	$366.00	$311.40	$351.30	$326.10	$501.30
RCP (ORDER CARDS)	$171.00	$252.30	$184.05	$172.05	$230.40	$210.60
INPUT NEW RECORDS	$52.80	$76.50	$125.00	$183.60	$167.45	$161.70
WLN RECON INPUT	$224.50	$0.00	$1,125.70	$142.00	$1,235.00	$20.80
CATALOG CARDS	$209.60	$309.76	$235.12	$232.72	$290.32	$252.24
TERMINAL MAINTENANCE	$125.00	$125.00	$125.00	$125.00	$125.00	$125.00
TERMINAL CONNECT CHARGE	$1,000.00	$1,000.00	$1,000.00	$1,000.00	$1,000.00	$1,000.00
CATALOGING TOTAL	$4,116.50	$4,819.29	$5,885.87	$5,231.52	$6,253.67	$5,058.64

Serials Retrospective Conversion: Project Design and In-House Implementation

Ruth Christ
Selina Lin

SUMMARY. Many factors must be considered in designing a serials retrospective conversion project. Based on their experience with a project deriving records from RLIN and entering records directly into a local NOTIS system, the authors discuss the project design considerations, authority control, recataloging issues, and clean-up problems and solutions. They compare the merits of methods employed in different phases of the project as well as on-going conversion. In converting all currently received serials not cataloged on RLIN, nearly 11,000 fully cataloged and 7,000 uncataloged titles were added to the University of Iowa database.

Contemplating the prospect of launching into a serials retrospective conversion project is enough to send a serials department into cycles of high anticipation and great dread. Neither is totally unwarranted. The benefits of having serials on-line are abundant. In many libraries, patron access to serials holdings records in the manual environment is quite limited. Protection of the records from loss or unauthorized alteration and ready patron access to current data are not compatible. Where an information desk is staffed, service may be limited by budget constraints. Maintaining up-to-date card catalogs is very labor intensive and book catalogs are out of date immediately. Having updated information appear instantaneously is a real

Ruth Christ is Serials Cataloging Unit Head and Selina Lin is Serials Cataloger at the University of Iowa Libraries, The University of Iowa, Iowa City, IA 52242.

51

"high" for cataloging personnel after years of dealing with card pulling, missing cards, revisions, typos, proofreading, and refiling. Arcane filing rules are replaced by indexing algorithms and even major changes don't involve refiling. Any serials cataloger, having recataloged a title for the "nth" time in a single year, will appreciate the move out of the manual environment.

Other benefits relate to additional opportunities in circulation for tailoring loan periods to different materials and patron categories. For serials, the ratio of volumes to titles is a great deal higher than that for monographs; conversion of a serial title represents, therefore, even greater circulation potential.

Many benefits accrue to having all formats on-line, but in acquisitions there are particular benefits that are even greater for serials. Claims and inquiries to publishers and vendors can be handled more expeditiously. As with missing catalog cards, missing Kardexes (order/receipt records) become a thing of the past. On-line check-in, on the other hand, may be a mixed blessing. Depending on the particular system being used, automated check-in may initially be more time-consuming than manual check-in was. Nonetheless, patrons and public services personnel seem to appreciate the display of current receipts. The increasing availability of predictive check-in is also a bright spot on the horizon.

The dread on the part of serials personnel comes from their appreciation of the saying that compares working with serials to untangling the yarn basket after the kitten has been playing. A strand pulled on here is tied to two over there which in turn are wrapped around several others and end in a knot. Even if the project will be comprehensive enough to include all the titles eventually, these entanglements disrupt an orderly linear progression and can generate piles of questions and problems to be worked on later as a part of clean-up.

We will first look at a variety of project design considerations, using as a point of reference the serials retrospective conversion project preparatory to the implementation of a NOTIS system at the University of Iowa in 1988. Then, various phases of the project will be described and contrasted and clean-up problems addressed.

PROJECT DESIGN CONSIDERATIONS

When initiating a serials retrospective conversion project, a number of questions need to be addressed before the project can begin:

1. What will the scope of the project be?

One of the first questions to be answered must be the coverage of the project. Is the goal to convert the whole collection in one project? Is a particular subset needed more urgently? Would a pilot project be beneficial? Breaking the project into sections makes the establishment of time lines easier and has positive implications for maintaining staff morale. Grant funding may relate to a particular subject area and thereby define the scope.

While most of the staff at Iowa agreed that it would be highly desirable to convert all serials titles (estimated at 93,000), a realistic compromise limited the initial project to those titles which would be needed by the Acquisitions Unit to provide for all the types of acquisitions records they would have to process. We decided to begin with a pilot project to get a feel for the types of problems we would encounter and the rate at which we could expect to progress. As time and resources permit, continuing conversion will cover non-standing order series which have volumes added or require recataloging for any reason. Another targeted group are those titles covered by the new on-line index databases.

2. How many of each type of record need to be converted?

In order to determine the magnitude of the project, a study needs to be conducted to quantify the projected conversion effort. By taking a small sampling of the records in the order file, we estimated that there were over 11,000 full bibliographic records and 8,000 provisional records to be converted. Our sampling was smaller than ideal but we were willing to accept a rough estimate rather than spend more time doing the count. The project would go forward in any case.

3. Should the records parallel those in the manual system or would any new types or levels of records be advantageous?

Typically, the first round of conversion to an on-line system is to transpose the current manual card format to the same display on a screen. Display is not a particular issue for designing a conversion project since the MARC format can be manipulated in various display formats depending on the software. Of more concern are the files of acquisitions records for uncataloged materials and memberships hitherto unavailable to the public. What are the consequences of making these records available? If they are to be made available to the public, should they be in a fuller form? Is there an option to suppress display of records?

We definitely wanted to maintain high quality records for our fully cataloged materials. For the other records, the order file provided little information beyond author (if any) and title. Obviously, access opportunities would be increased since access would not be limited to a single point. The need for cross references would decrease proportionately. Because the minimum needed to create a bibliographic record on a NOTIS system is a title (MARC 245), we could create very minimal provisional records for materials not fully cataloged. The types of records needed for acquisitions purposes had not changed with automation, so we decided to go ahead with the creation of those records. Any new categories could be added as the need arose. At the time of our project, the suppression of record display was not yet an option.

4. What are the bibliographic standards level of the existing manual records and the standards level of the desired end product?

If the converted records are eventually to be loaded into a national database, bibliographic standards must be met or the records must at least be coded non-standard. Conversion of line-o-dex type records would require much data from external sources to create full records. Is a component of the project to be raising minimal records to full standard? Must the final records be consistent with AACR2 or is cataloging which was done to standard at the time of creation acceptable? Must all "latest title" records be updated to successive entry records?

For decades, serials at the University of Iowa have been fully cataloged to national standards following Library of Congress rule interpretations (with the exception of a several year delay in implementing successive entry cataloging). The records have been maintained to reflect title changes, numbering inconsistencies, etc. Thus, we had the choice of deriving records from RLIN or entering our records "as is" (and, in fact, we ultimately used both approaches). We have also followed a policy of recataloging only when some change in the publication called for it, not just because rules changed. Thus, we have numerous well-behaved older serials with titles like "Bulletin" which might actually carry a title like "Quarterly bulletin of the XYZ Association." We will look at how we dealt with some of these specific problems later.

Because our journals are unclassified and many are in storage due to overcrowding in our stacks, complete conversion to successive entry or even to AACR2 form of title would have added enormously to the workload. This might also have been an appropriate time to classify, but there was unquestionably inadequate staff available to consider this. On the other hand, since corporate entries would be under authority control, those which were not in AACR2 form would be a constant source of conflict unless updated. We decided that it would be worthwhile to bring this small set of records up to AACR2 form. For classified titles, we also decided that conversion from latest title to successive entry records would be desirable in view of the fact that no reshelving would be required.

5. What effects would the public display of certain processing records have?

In the manual file it was possible to maintain acquisitions records for samples, discards, memberships, and vertical file materials without making these available to the public. Will the display of records for samples and discards raise false expectations or perhaps some concern on the part of the public? How can possible confusion on the part of patrons be avoided? Are appropriate on-line messages available and sufficient? Should display of these records be suppressed if possible?

Our practice has varied over the years regarding the representation of Cat. Sep. (cataloged and classified separately) series in the public catalog. At one time, we used a single card explaining that each item was classified separately and that a contents listing could be found in the Serials Department. Later, we filed added entries in the public catalog instead of keeping a contents listing. The on-line display would combine the advantages of each method.

As for the other types, display of records for samples and discards caused some uneasiness on the part of the staff. Because the records could be coded to display the message "For staff use," it was decided that the advantages of having all ordering and receiving on-line outweighed the possible confusion that might arise. It is now possible to code records in NOTIS for suppression from public display, a reminder that in the fluid situation of conversion, decisions are not necessarily permanent, but merely reflect the best options available at a particular point in time.

6. Should the conversion be done in-house or should an outside vendor be utilized?

Several factors need to be considered. Cost and speed are to be investigated if a commercial vendor is being considered. Also, the amount of preprocessing and post-conversion clean-up might vary with different vendors. As mentioned above, the standards level of the manual records needs to be considered. Skeletal records or those which have not been maintained would have the least conflicting information when compared to an outside database. These would be most readily converted by an outside vendor. Obviously an institution which had not previously fully cataloged its journals, for instance, would greatly benefit from derived records and could probably work with a vendor to great advantage. Well-maintained records are likely to have more information than many of the records in an outside database and thus there would be more potential for losing some of that information. After listening to various discussions, we were inclined to follow conventional wisdom and didn't seriously consider using an outside-vendor option.

7. If done in-house, should records be derived from a national database or should existing records be keyed directly into the local database?

Unless the library is linked to a national database and has implemented a local database or is at least considering doing so, this question is irrelevant. Even if both systems are in place, this question is still not easily answered because of the trade-offs. Some obvious advantages to deriving from a national database are the additional information that can be obtained, such as ISSNs, publishing history (e.g., absorptions and ceases) which may have been missed, updated name and subject headings, etc., and the reduction of data entry and associated proofreading. Other factors in this decision would be relative costs, experience level of available staff, and cooperative commitments. Availability of funds for additional on-line searching or for additional staff must be weighed against availability of existing staff. These and other questions will be dealt with in subsequent sections.

The conversion project at the University of Iowa consisted of phases using each method. At the time we wanted to begin our conversion project, our local system had not yet been implemented. Our options were to begin by deriving records from RLIN or to wait several months. The desire to have at least one block of records completely on-line for acquisitions testing purposes as soon as the local system was brought up made the choice for phase 1 rather clear. We would begin by deriving records from RLIN.

One unexpected discovery we made was that, aside from the actual data entry, it is not necessarily easier to derive records than to enter them from scratch. We had learned from our monographic conversion project that data entry of original records is more easily handled by lower level staff than deriving records because of the greater degree of decision making involved in the latter. Because of the living nature of serials, many changes occur which could result in necessary modifications to the cataloging. In addition, like most libraries, we must rely on lower level staff to perform serials check-in, and since this is the staff with the most opportunity to notice problems or variations, much depends on how well trained and observant this staff is. High turnover and the speed at which this staff may be expected to work are also factors, as is local policy on what variations warrant recataloging. Because notes are optional, libraries may only choose to update records for specific categories of changes. At Iowa, we note errors in numbering involving whole volumes, but do not generally make note of numbering errors on single issues within a volume except in our receiving record. We also do not attempt to note changes in imprint unless necessary to prevent confusion between two like titles. Series statements were faithfully recorded for many years until staff reductions forced us to cut back on the tracking of Cat. Sep. series. Again, our delay in implementing successive entry cataloging made us "out of sync" in some cases. Many differences between our own records and those from RLIN required decisions which less-experienced project staff could not easily be trained to make. It was more expedient to have student workers tag and enter the existing records than to have full-time staff compare those records with RLIN MARC records, evaluate the differences, and revise the records.

Concern was expressed about upholding our commitment to RLIN if we did direct entry into OASIS (the local NOTIS system), but we were reassured that a tape-loading program was being developed which would allow us to send all of these additional local records to RLIN. This has, in fact, recently occurred.

8. If done in-house, which classification levels of staff should be involved and who will be available?

Are there funds for additional project staff or will the staff come from internal reassignment? Will any experienced personnel be available? The level of staff needed will depend partially on how much recataloging is incorporated into the conversion process. It is very difficult to refrain from recataloging, but the more recataloging done, the higher the staff level needed. This can be a spiralling situation in that the more highly trained the staff is, the more they will see that could or should be done.

We found that it took more highly-trained staff to deal with derived records than it did to tag and enter our local records directly. Our project team consisted of two permanent serials catalogers who also had regular duties, two temporary professionals who were drafted part-time from the monographic conversion project, .1 FTE temporary Library Assistant III[1] and .4 FTE Library Assistant IV who did searching for bibliographic records, 1.5 FTE library school students who did tagging, and 3.5 FTE other students who did inputting, card-pulling, photocopying, proofreading, and other miscellaneous tasks. Holdings were done by 1 FTE clerk-typist on loan from Binding, our own added volumes personnel (.25 FTE Library Assistant II) and .75 FTE student assistants.

9. Will all records be converted in one pass, or are there logical groups into which the records could be divided?

Some factors to be considered are: If both fully cataloged records and skeletal or provisional records are to be entered, are the standards and procedures different enough to cause confusion if done in one pass? Is there a more pressing need for a certain category to be done so that testing, for instance, may proceed? Is a holdings format available? Or, is a major change about to occur which might make it desirable to leave entry of holdings until later?

We processed our full and provisional records at the same time, but each category was done by different personnel because of significant differences in training requirements. The holdings were done in an entirely separate pass at a later time so that we could concentrate our initial efforts on preparing the bibliographic records necessary to provide the base for bringing up the acquisitions module. If we were just beginning our project now, we would certainly wait for the MARC Format for Holdings to be implemented on NOTIS to avoid going through an electronic conversion process.

10. What level of authority control will be applied to the converted records?

Here again, one's relationship with a bibliographic utility might impose certain requirements. Also, the decision to use or not use external authority processing will be a factor. What provisions will there be in the local system for conflict and error detection?

For derived records, we did no authority work except for certain geographic main entries, such as universities, which were highly likely to have changed. For direct input records, only corporate entries were checked. Few personal names occur in our serials records. Eventually all of our records were processed by UTLAS, and any overlooked authority problems were reported to us. Fortunately, this turned out to be a very small number. The main problem we encountered relating to authority control pertained to binding. For classified titles, we could simply update the binding entry to reflect name changes and not worry about differences on the spines since shelving would not be affected. The unclassified journals, shelved alphabetically by main entry, were another matter. Most of our departmental libraries are very crowded and would find any major reshelving projects impossible. In addition, many volumes have had to be sent to storage. Our current solution to this situation is to leave these volumes shelved under the old main entry and use "shelved-as" notes in our holdings records.

One aspect of authority control which generated a clean-up project is series authorities. Here we find that AACR2 forms and successive title records are more critical issues if the series records, the series tracings, and the authority records are to come together online. This topic will be addressed further in the section on clean-up.

11. What are the available funds and how do they correlate with the desired project needs?

For a number of years libraries which could identify sizable unique collections were often able to obtain grant funding for retrospective conversion projects. When retrospective conversion was the hot topic, it seemed that grant funds were more readily available than they are now, when interest has shifted to preservation. As more collections are converted, it is harder to identify blocks of titles of wide interest which will appeal to grants agencies. Very specialized collections may appeal to agencies which share an interest in that specialty. In this era of extremely tight budgets, there may well not be an available budget line to support added expenses for project staff, external processing, etc. For this reason, more libraries are likely to have to absorb the expense of any conversion into their operating budgets.

In our case, funds generated from RLG monographic projects provided for additional professional staff for the first several months of our project. The remainder of the project had to be carried out by permanent staff and student assistants. This placed a heavy burden on the staff to avoid being buried under a double load.

12. How much recataloging will be done in the process of conversion? What are the implications for clean-up?

For serials, there can easily be a question of whether to call the project recataloging or conversion. No matter how carefully records are maintained, it seems that numerous things are overlooked which could be noted in the bibliographic records. Is it worthwhile spending the time to incorporate all of the information available in the national databases into one's local records? Probably not, but where should the line be drawn? Certainly it is useful to know that a title has ceased or has been absorbed by another title. It may be less vital to record the fact that v. 27, no. 3 was accidentally called v. 27, no. 2. Recataloging slows the process of conversion. It takes considerable time to evaluate the accuracy and necessity of additional information. As mentioned above, we discovered that there was a definite tradeoff between thoroughness and speed when dealing with derived records.

One serious implication of not recataloging is limiting access. As mentioned previously, many titles cataloged under old rules appear in a truncated form under a corporate heading, e.g., "American Chemical Society. Journal." This creates a problem for access when one searches under the full title: Journal of the American Chemical Society. To compensate for this shortcoming without recataloging all titles done in this fashion, a provisional title access field (NOTIS 924) was added to spell out the full title, and a note (NOTIS 940) was also added: Title in 924 used: < date- >. Over time, we hope that many of these records will be fully recataloged as other routine maintenance brings them to a cataloger's attention. Adding access points to these converted records has become part of the clean-up process for Serials Control and Cataloging staff.

As much as we tried to avoid recataloging, there were times when we seemed to have no choice but to proceed. Identified authority conflicts were usually dealt with immediately to avoid wasted effort. If a corporate main entry needed to be updated, we would also evaluate the possibility of a shift to title main entry, applying current rules, before having new binding records and shelf list cards made. Some problems were deemed larger than we cared to deal with in the course of the main project and were set aside for more careful attention as a part of clean-up. In the direct-entry phase of the project, analyzed serials done as latest title records fell into this category. These were generally entered as is for the sake of acquisitions needs with the understanding that they would probably be split into successive records in a series authorities clean-up project.

IMPLEMENTATION OF THE PROJECT PHASES

Background

New serial titles had been entered on RLIN since 1980. In addition, manual titles needing recataloging were entered on-line, so that over a period of several years many titles had been converted on demand. These on-line records could be readily loaded into OASIS as soon as the system was brought up and testing was completed. This occurred at the end of June 1988. The decision to implement the NOTIS acquisitions module mandated having all currently received serials on-line. Our first goal was to have a pilot group of these records available for acquisitions activity at the beginning of the fiscal year, July 1, 1988. The K-M portion of the alphabet was arbitrarily selected for the pilot project.

The initial retrospective conversion project was intended to include only the remaining serials needing on-line bibliographic records on which to build acquisitions records. Locations could be supplied from the cards used for conversion, but holdings presented such a complex mass of data that we decided to deal with them in a separate pass after the more urgently needed bibliographic records were completed. In addition to fully cataloged materials, records were created for other serials on standing order or regularly received as gifts. Among these latter categories were Cat. Seps., samples, discards, and vertical file materials. Government documents were not included because they are ordered and received in a separate department.

For ease in managing workflow, separate procedures were set up for processing fully-cataloged serials and the categories for which skeletal records were deemed to be sufficient. As mentioned above, holdings were also done as a separate procedure.

Identification of Records for Conversion

Each drawer of the visible file (Kardex) was photocopied (Figure 1). This gave us manageable lists which could be carried to other locations without disturbing the check-in process and on which notes could be made.

A template was created which included fixed fields and holdings fields and provided a place to insert a card. To create the template, printouts of the fixed fields and holdings screens were first photocopied and reduced so that when the card was inserted, the whole unit could be enlarged, returning it to standard-page size, but with space so that tags and indicators could be written next to the data on the card reproductions. Separate templates were produced for RLIN data entry and for OASIS data entry (Figure 2).

Entries already on-line were represented by easily identified computer-generated cards and were eliminated from the list as students pulled the public catalog main entry cards. The students pulled the cards in small batches, leaving oversize cards in their place rather than the customary typed temporary slips. Each card in turn was inserted into the space in the template and photocopied and enlarged in one step. Any tracings on the backs of cards were also copied and enlarged. The cards were then immediately refiled so the public would have essentially uninterrupted access to all titles.

The worksheets were divided into three levels of difficulty which came to be referred to as "the good, the bad, and the ugly." Level One consisted of straightforward records with no apparent complexities. Level Two consisted of records with title changes or simple relationships with other titles such as supplements or absorption. Level Three consisted of the more complex records with problems such as mergers or dashed-on supplements. Samples of many different types of situations were set aside for training.

While the photocopying continued, training of the project cataloging personnel began with three professional catalogers who had little or no previous serials experience. Since they had been previously working on monographic conversion, the training consisted primarily of learning some of the basic differences between monographic and serials cataloging and those fields peculiar to serials records. We hoped eventually to shift some of the work to library assistants and students as their roles in the monographic conversion project ended, but most of them left the university because of graduation and better jobs so they were not available.

Phase 1: Deriving from a National Database
January-March 1988

At the time we decided to begin our serials retrospective conversion project in early 1988, we had not yet loaded our RLIN records into a local database. Because we wanted to be able to begin before the database would be available, we chose to do the pilot project on RLIN. We anticipated that this would also provide the added benefit of fuller bibliographic information and AACR2 forms of entries. We also felt that we could bypass authority searching when using full standard records and rely on authority processing by UTLAS, a Canadian vendor, to catch the odd problem.

Searching on RLIN was done primarily by the Library Assistant IV who already did our regular searching, so it was not necessary to give him any further training. He was assisted on the Level One records by a temporary Library Assistant III from the monographic

FIGURE 1. Portion of a Visible File Drawer

Music	Kirchenmusiker.
Bot-Add Vol	Kirkia.
Main	Kirtlandia.
Ref-Add Call	Kiryat sefer (Jerusalem)
Main	Kiva.
Sep	Kivung special publication.

FIGURE 2. Tagged Worksheet for Direct Entry on OASIS

```
                                          NOTIS CATALOGING
UL#          FMT S RT a BL s DT          R/DT none     STAT nn E/L 1 DCF     D/S D
SRC d PLACE nyu LANG eng MOD   OA   REPRO   S/STAT c DT/1 1967 DT/2 9999
CONT        S/T    FREQ u REG u MED    GOVT    TPA u IA u CIA u ISDS    CONF 0 SLE 1
          040   IaU‡cIaU
          043   n-us---

                                                            30570600

      Engineering 245 00
      T73   Engineering and technology enrollments.
      E495362 0b fall 1967-
          260 00 New York,‡bEngineering Manpower Commission
                 of Engineers Joint Council.
            300   v.‡c29cm.

                 Title varies: 247 10  Engineering and
              technician enrollments
                650 b0                              United States.
        650 b0    1. Engineering‡x Study and teaching‡z U.S.
              2. Technical education‡z U.S. United States. 710 20 I. Engineers
              Joint Council.‡b Engineering Manpower Commission.
              II. Title: Engin-     eering and technician
              enrollments.                         IaU 75 JEC

UL SERL   S/STAT ? FREQ ? S/T

STATUS h DT            AD
NOTES SL
001 2L CN engn/1 ‡kFOLIO ‡bT73 ‡c.E495
    NOTES

002 2  CN
    NOTES
003 2  CN
    NOTES
004 2  CN
    NOTES
005 2  CN
    NOTES
006 2  CN
```

retrospective conversion project. In cases where we had latest title cataloging and the RLIN records were done successively, he was instructed to print not only successive records for classified titles, but also the best available latest title records for unclassified titles with title changes, leaving the decision of which to use to the catalogers.

Beginning with the Level One records, the catalogers compared the worksheets created from photocopying the public catalog cards with the printouts of the RLIN records. Information found on our local records but not the RLIN records was tagged for addition to the derived record. By the time the Level One records were completed, the catalogers had gained enough confidence to deal with the additional fields and complexities of the Level Two records. When latest title records were replaced by successive records, students typed the necessary shelf list temps. In many cases, only the experienced catalogers were able to make decisions on Level Three records. The completed worksheets were passed to student typists who did the data entry on RLIN. Only one card to be used for proofreading was ordered for each title unless the main entry was changed. In that case, replacement cards were also ordered and the worksheets were set aside to initiate update of the binding records.

In part due to a change in the searching rate structure at RLIN, it was decided that the remainder of the Kardex titles would be converted on the local database after it was installed in late June 1988. This was deemed feasible because the University of Iowa Libraries has a long tradition of outstanding cataloging. One category would continue to be input on RLIN. That consisted of the Chinese, Japanese, and Korean titles (ca. 150). These had to be done on the RLIN CJK terminal in order to retain the vernacular portions of the records since OASIS does not have that capability. All other non-roman titles were romanized and processed with the main body of records.

Between mid-March and June 1988, the temporary catalogers returned to the monographic conversion project in order to facilitate clean-up there. The serials catalogers worked on clean-up from the first phase of the serials conversion project, on planning for the Kardex conversion to OASIS order/pay/receipt records for the K-M pilot group, and on planning for the phases involving direct entry on the local system for full and provisional bibliographic records and holdings records. During this period, the students continued photocopying Kardex drawers and creating worksheets using a new template matching NOTIS fixed fields and holdings screens. By June, all the catalogers had returned to the serials conversion project to begin tagging in order to build up a reserve of records for entry by the typists.

Phase 2: Direct Conversion on Local System
July 1988 to February 1989

As soon as all of the 1980-June 1988 RLIN data tapes were loaded to create the new OASIS database, entry of both the full and provisional records began. These were done simultaneously by different teams. The creation of the provisional records will be described in a separate section following the discussion relating to the full bibliographic records.

Three catalogers worked on tagging the worksheets for full bibliographic records. In this phase all data elements needed to be tagged and all of the appropriate fixed fields had to be filled in since no searching was done on RLIN and thus no records were derived. The catalogers determined that they could only tag an average of 30 records a day each without affecting consistency, accuracy, and morale. This meant that we would have over 5,000 records left to tag when the grant funds supporting the two temporary librarians were exhausted. Attempts to secure additional funds were unsuccessful, so an alternate plan went into effect.

By October 1988, the last two grant-funded temporary full-time retrospective conversion positions had expired, leaving only students and two permanent librarians to carry out the project. Four library school students were trained to do MARC tagging. From September to December 1988, these student taggers were able to complete the remainder of the 10,000 records which had been transferred from manual catalog cards to worksheets via the template described earlier. Besides tagging, these and five other students also performed a variety of other duties such as data entry, proofreading, and authority searching to reduce monotony. Basically, all manual records were entered on-line exactly the way they were cataloged. Latest title records were not upgraded. The typists completed their work in February 1989.

Authority searching was limited to corporate name headings in main and added entries. Some obviously outdated subject headings and subdivisions were also changed; e.g., U.S. to United States, Yearbooks to Periodicals; or omitted, e.g., Collected works. If a conflict was found, the student searcher would make the appropriate change on the tagged worksheet before it was input. One card was ordered for each converted title for proofreading purposes.

If no correction was necessary, the machine-produced card was exchanged for the manual card in the serials catalog, and all manual cards for that title were pulled from the public catalog. In the case of an altered main entry, a few more steps would follow. For classified titles, a new card set was ordered to replace the manual cards for all locations involved, and a new binding record was made to match the on-line bibliographic record. For unclassified titles, in order to avoid massive relabeling and reshelving caused by authority conflict in the main entry, the note "Shelved as: [old heading]" was added to the volume holdings screen. The same information was also added to the binding record to prevent confusion. This is not the best long-term solution, but was the only manageable solution under the circumstances.

COMPARISON OF PHASE 1 AND PHASE 2

At the end of phase 1, we were very pleased with the speed of the processing (1,053 records, including clean-up, in seven weeks) and the quality of the end product. We were especially happy to be adding many useful access points, particularly those found in records derived from Library of Congress copy. In addition to ISSNs, these records often contained title variations that were important in machine indexing. We discovered that several titles had ceased or suspended publication and passed that information on to the Acquisitions Unit. Our main concern was that we were relying on heavy involvement of high-level staff. Too many decisions required experienced staff who were already overloaded with regular duties in addition to the retrospective conversion project. Another concern we had was that, on an ongoing basis, after the initial tape load, there would be about a two-week delay before records cataloged on RLIN would appear in the local database.

When RLG announced an intent to change from charging for derives to charging for searches, it appeared that our costs would be adversely affected since our workflow called for one search to find suitable copy to make a printout for comparison with our local record, and a second search by the typist to retrieve the record in order to derive from it with our modifications. We were also informed that the terms of the temporary project librarians would not be extended beyond October 1988. To our dismay, we found that we really had no choice but to design a project using permanent staff and student assistants to directly enter our existing records into the local database as soon as it became available.

Once we began actually working on phase 2, however, we began to see that the task was not as formidable as we had feared and that there were even some advantages to the new process. Foremost was the possibility of immediate record creation to facilitate on-line order/pay/receipt and check-in processing by serials staff. There was no delay waiting for a tape load from RLIN. Fewer decisions regarding recataloging needed to be made, making it possible to rely mainly on student assistants to carry out the project, thereby reducing cost as well as stress on the permanent staff. These students could be paid out of funds already available, while using RLIN would have required additional funds due to the newly announced searching charge.

We were rather concerned about the data entry aspect of phase 2 since all fields would have to be entered instead of editing existing records. We were fortunate to have students who were proficient typists, and found that in many ways it was easier to type a new record than it was to find and edit an existing record. This may not have been the case with slower typists. Proofreading was also a concern. By limiting the close proofreading to access points, other students were able to do this task quite quickly.

One thing the two phases and the following holdings project had in common was the heavy burden placed on the two permanent serials catalogers working on the project to solve problems, monitor quality, keep students motivated, plan the next steps, and do at least a token amount of regular cataloging. Our third permanent serials cataloger kept processing as much as possible of the regular cataloging. In view of the fact that additional experienced staff was not affordable, a slower pace would have been desirable though we must admit that the pace was partially self-inflicted. We wanted to see the project done right, and instantly!

HOLDINGS

Holdings were added to the converted records in a separate project. When the cards generated for proofreading in the bibliographic conversion were exchanged for the manual serials catalog main entry cards, the holdings cards, which were filed behind the main entry cards, were also pulled. Much discussion was held about the format for the holdings. In the end, the advocates of national standards prevailed, and we developed a format following the American National Standard for Serial Holdings Statements, ANSI Z39.44, level 3 with some detail at level 4 so that we could be more specific about incomplete volumes. In order to retain the correlation between enumeration and chronology, we made separate summary lines for each decade when applicable. This was done as a compromise between giving a single summary of all holdings for brevity and listing individual items for clarity. Proofreading the holdings has proven to be a daunting task for which we have been unable to allocate sufficient time due to our effort to catch up with our regular cataloging. We assume that most factual, if not format, errors will come to light when our barcoding project is carried out.

PROCEDURE FOR CREATING PROVISIONAL RECORDS

In a separate procedure, provisional records (with only a title and, when appropriate, corporate entry field) were created for all uncataloged Kardex titles for acquisitions purposes. These included samples, discards, memberships, Cat. Seps., vertical file materials, etc. Two students were trained to search the authority file on OASIS whenever necessary (e.g., Cat. Sep. series and corporate names) and input these short records. In total, they entered 6,414 provisional records.

Phase 3: Clean-Up and Beyond

Several categories of records were identified as being sufficiently problematic to warrant setting aside for later processing or processing by experienced serials catalogers. Among these were records which had dashed-on supplements. These had to be looked at carefully to determine whether the supplements required a separate record or could be incorporated into a note on the main work.

Records for which corporate main entries needed to be converted to AACR2 forms were entered using the new form, with a printout being saved to prompt further action. Using these printouts, binding records were updated, and as described above, "shelved-as" notes were recorded as appropriate.

As implementation of on-line check-in progressed, acquisitions personnel were asked to bounce any issues bearing an ISSN for which one did not display in the record. They were also asked to bounce issues of any title which they did not readily find on OASIS. Sometimes indexing peculiarities make it difficult to find a title, so we try to add access points when possible. In order to maintain standard records, these access points are often added in local fields. Our assumption is that if the staff can't find something, we can't expect the public to find it either.

Some of the categories of provisional records were identified as undesirable for public display. Since the first phases of our conversion project, NOTIS has added a field which will allow suppression of display to the public. Discards and most membership records are now being coded for suppression.

In the pilot project, there was no authority control effort due to the expectation of UTLAS authority processing. Once that processing was done, electronically generated reports identified errors for correction.

Clean-up of converted bibliographic records has become a routine procedure because of the fluid nature of serials. Many missed title changes, extra access points (added parallel titles, acronyms, variant forms of a title, etc.), when spotted by serials control or check-in staff, are referred to catalogers for corrective action. With basic records on-line, recataloging is much easier than in the manual environment.

While UTLAS processing could identify problems with form of entry, it did not identify conflicts between authority records and serial bibliographic records on choice of entry. Some serials needed conversion to title main entry rather than to a new form of corporate main entry. We would like to systematically verify that each analyzed serial coordinates with a series authority record and that the heading use codes and tracing practice codes are set properly.

CURRENT STATUS

While we still had the experienced students, we extended the project to include all of the in-process materials on the catalogers' shelves, both maintenance and new titles. Ideally, the entire serials collection should be converted if only to facilitate future automated circulation. However, due to limited resources, we can only convert currently received government publications and titles that happen to need maintenance or cataloging attention, e.g., non-standing order added volumes, ceases, suspensions, and title changes. In short, the continuing conversion is basically acquisitions- and maintenance-driven. Once the circulation function is automated, conversion will undoubtedly be driven also by circulation.

GTO (Generic Transfer and Overlay) became available to us in December 1990, making conversion much easier. In this process records are downloaded directly from RLIN into OASIS. All manually cataloged titles that need to be converted are now searched on RLIN and copy found is GTO'ed to OASIS to be edited in the local database. Recataloging from latest to successive entry for classified serials has become a routine practice. GTO speeds up the workflow considerably and we can again take advantage of on-line shared cataloging, thereby greatly enhancing the content of our bibliographic records. If GTO had been available earlier, our retrospective conversion project might have been done quite differently.

CONCLUSION

By doing the serials retrospective conversion project in-house, using a national utility in the pilot, and only the local database in the main project, we were able to compare the advantages and disadvantages of the two methods. It became quite clear early on that deriving from a national database and editing records requires a higher level of staff than entering manual records from scratch directly on local database. Training students to tag was easier than training full-time staff to make editing decisions when deriving from other libraries' copy. On the other hand, it was not realistic to expect student proofreaders to catch all errors no matter how thorough they were. Fortunately (or unfortunately!), by their very nature serials require continuing attention, resulting in the detection and correction of many errors by full-time staff. The most important step is getting the records on-line. All other automated functions become possible only when the bibliographic record is on-line. Making all of these functions possible is the most rewarding aspect of the project.

NOTE

1. At the University of Iowa, Library Assistant positions have four classes, I through IV, with IV being at the top of the range.

Workflow Considerations
in Retrospective Conversion Projects
for Scores

Michelle Koth
Laura Gayle Green

SUMMARY. Complexities of music materials and the uniform titles and subject headings for them make score retrospective conversion an expensive and time-demanding venture. Careful pre-recon planning and workflow development are therefore important in score recon projects. The workflows from seven score recon projects with details of staffing levels and perceived advantages and disadvantages

Michelle Koth is Catalog Librarian at the Yale University Music Library. From 1987 to 1990, she was Retrospective Conversion Librarian at the Indiana University Music Library as part of the Associated Music Libraries Group (AMLG)-sponsored recon grant. Previously, she had been involved with retrospective conversion activities at Bowling Green State University.

Laura Gayle Green is Visiting Assistant Librarian, Music Cataloger at the Indiana University Music Library for the Associated Music Libraries Group recon grant.

This article was first given as a presentation by Michelle Koth at an informal session on retrospective conversion at the Music OCLC Users Group Meeting, February 1990, Tucson, AZ, and was expanded into article form with the editorial assistance of Laura Gayle Green.

are presented. Pre-recon considerations–source of cataloging information, what to convert, in what order to convert, the level of staffing, and
the issue of when and how to do authority work–are discussed in relation to the seven workflows.

Faced with the task of converting their collections, librarians look
to the experiences of other libraries when planning and developing
procedures for this overwhelming job. Music librarians, however,
will find little subject-specific guidance in the library literature.
Articles for book recon simply do not address the complexities of
converting music materials. For example, Finn says that "[biblio-
graphic] matches [for books] can be achieved with very brief bibliographic information if you are willing to accept a match in the
broadest possible terms, i.e., the same title and publication date."[1]
Even without taking authority work into consideration, score recon
is far more complex because of the intricacies of music publishing.
The same musical work can be issued in various manifestations
over the course of decades or even centuries. As a result, one work
can be published with variant forms of title in different languages,
in different formats (study score, vocal score, conductor's score,
parts, etc.), and with different plate or publisher's numbers. Problems with copyright and publication dates arise when the work is
reprinted by another publisher or even when reissued by the same
publisher. Variations in title on the cover, title page, and caption
can result in several bibliographic records for the same item.
　　There are few articles[2] relating the experiences of libraries which
have converted music materials. This article will discuss pre-con-
version considerations which affect planning workflow and staffing,
and will present workflows from recon projects at seven libraries,
along with the perceptions of staff from each library on the advantages and disadvantages of each workflow.

PRE-CONVERSION CONSIDERATIONS

Heitshu and Quinn list three basic decisions for planning recon:
what will be converted; in what order will it be converted; and what
will be the source of cataloging information.[3] As a means of identi-

fying what to convert, Finn suggests taking an inventory in the planning stages of the project. An inventory can reveal the percentage of the collection that is missing and can be used to make decisions about items to be withdrawn prior to conversion, as well as to establish the amount of useable information existing on cards. DiCarlo and Maxfield[4] also recommend a pre-recon sample of the collection to determine if an inventory of the entire collection, or perhaps only sections of it, would avoid the cost of converting records for missing items. Areas of suspected high loss could be targeted for inventory.

To estimate the percentage of titles requiring original cataloging, Peterson advises searching a sample of titles to be converted in the database.[5] Records found in the database can then be evaluated for quality and completeness of cataloging. This evaluation can provide an indication of the level of staff needed to edit these records.

Deciding on the order of conversion can be influenced by the awareness of what has been converted by the major music recon and cataloging projects and which databases contain these records. Since 1985, the Associated Music Libraries Group (AMLG) has sponsored a Title II-C funded coordinated score recon effort to convert the holdings of six libraries spanning LC Class M and the scores in class MT, targeting the strengths of the six libraries' collections.[6] The AMLG recon records[7] have been cross-loaded into OCLC and RLIN, and thus are available to users of either database. Additionally, approximately 3,000 headings (primarily name headings) established as part of the AMLG project have been contributed to the LC authority file through the NACO Music Project.[8] The effects that the AMLG grant has had on OCLC and RLIN and that the NACO Music Project will have on authority work have not been assessed. Both projects will undoubtedly make music recon and the necessary upgrade of headings easier for other libraries, as was the intent of both projects. The Research Libraries Group (RLG) has also sponsored a recon project, conducted solely on RLIN. Their grant funding enabled the UC-Berkeley and Yale University music libraries to spend three years converting scores (M and MT) and books (ML385-ML410). Indiana University, as part of the first year of its Title II-C Opera Grant, completed one year of cataloging of nineteenth-century French opera vocal scores on

OCLC. Being aware of these and similar projects and their current status can be a factor in planning what to convert and in what order.

Choosing the source of cataloging information will be based in part on which is more complete, the shelflist card or the main entry card. One consideration is whether enough information is found on the card to successfully search for a match and convert the item. The disruption resulting from pulling cards from either catalog is another factor in this decision. At this point in the planning stage, the length of time the cards will be out of the catalog should be considered, and the alternatives the staff will have in performing shelflist activities or the public in locating items being converted should be evaluated.

The level of staff required to convert will be determined partly by the level of conversion the library will do: strict recon, with database cleanup done later, or recon "bordering on recataloging rather than strict conversion."[9] Peterson, in discussing serials conversion, says "by definition, [recon] does not involve cataloging or recataloging of materials, although some recataloging is usually necessary."[10] With score bibliographic records, some recataloging is frequently necessary to make the records more complete and useful. Given the changes AACR2 has caused in headings, most records also require the upgrading of name and uniform title headings. If music bibliographic records are to be completely accurate at the time of conversion, then a knowledgeable staff is needed to select the correct record on the utility and to upgrade or add necessary access points. If the goal is to convert the score collection quickly and correct problems locally, then lower levels of staff may be able to convert music records. Minimal local information can be added to the bibliographic database and more crucial changes made in the local online environment. In this case, less training is needed to convert scores. Emphasis would be placed on the time and manner in which authority cleanup will be done.

If no new staff is to be hired to do music recon, can the existing staff be trained to do so? Music materials require special knowledge and experience to catalog and to convert. Jack Krantz describes how a library might train paraprofessionals to catalog music.[11] His article describes a situation with an extensive review process. Such a luxury rarely occurs when faced with the time limitations of a recon project.

INSTITUTIONAL WORKFLOWS

Workflow and staffing levels from seven recon projects are presented below. Each of the libraries include one or two aspects unique among the seven which helped determine workflow and staffing. The libraries are W. Frank Steely Library at Northern Kentucky University, Jerome Library at Bowling Green State University, Indiana University Music Library, Michigan State University Library, University of California-Berkeley Music Library, The Eda Kuhn Loeb Music Library at Harvard University, and the Cornell University Music Library. Northern Kentucky, Bowling Green, Indiana, and Michigan State are OCLC libraries; Indiana and Michigan State have enhance status[12] for scores. UC-Berkeley, Cornell, and Harvard are RLIN libraries and, along with Indiana, are involved in the AMLG recon project. Harvard converted its collection from the public catalog while the other six libraries used the shelflist. For the AMLG project, UC-Berkeley converted on RLIN one year and for two years contracted with OCLC to convert their scores. Northern Kentucky represents the case of the small library with its music collection forming part of the general collection. Both Northern Kentucky and Cornell used their shelflist cards as a basis for authority work before searching for bibliographic records. Bowling Green and Michigan State are mid-sized universities with separate music libraries. Both converted their music collections as part of a larger, library-wide conversion project. While Bowling Green did recon in-house, Michigan State contracted with OCLC to do their recon. The people who shared their workflow procedures and their perceptions of them are Perry Bratcher at Northern Kentucky, the Music Library staff and the Cataloging Department at Bowling Green, the authors for Indiana University, Mary Black-Shier and Sara Siebert at Michigan State, Jill Duerr at UC-Berkeley, Virginia Danielson at Harvard, and Donna Lester at Cornell.

The music collection at *Northern Kentucky University* is housed in the main library, which has a collection of 250,000 volumes. Out of 6,600 scores, 525 needed conversion. Their recon workflow is described in Perry Bratcher's article "Music OCLC Recon: The Practical Approach." Bratcher, who oversaw the general recon project and thus was involved with converting the scores, had a music background and did all current music cataloging at Northern Kentucky. He alone converted the scores, as the paraprofessional staff did not feel they could attain the necessary expertise in music cataloging. Also, as a policy, students do no inputting at Northern Kentucky. The project was grant-funded, and so speed in completing the project was essential. With four hours per week dedicated to it, score recon was completed in six months.

Workflow

1. Shelflist cards for items needing to be converted were pulled.
1a. Initially, the cards were taken to the stacks so that publisher and plate numbers could be noted on the cards, to help identify matches on OCLC (at this time the 028 field was not searchable on OCLC). This step was determined to be too time-consuming and was discontinued.
2. Authority work was completed before searching for bibliographic records. In order to save time, cards from each drawer were ordered alphabetically so that authority work could be batched by composer. The LC authority file was searched and the AACR2 form of headings, when found, was noted on the cards. The heading on the card was accepted when not found in the authority file, but matched the heading found later in the OCLC record. When a conflict arose, the heading on the card was used, unless the OCLC record was DLC/DLC. Many added entries, such as editor, arranger, etc., were deemed unnecessary, since sophisticated access to the catalog was not expected. When uniform titles were not found in the authority file, information on the card was accepted, unless the librarian knew the heading had changed or could make a quick guess as to the correct title.
3. The information was input, the update transactions completed, and the cards returned to the shelflist.

Advantages

1. By arranging cards from each drawer alphabetically by composer, authority work for uniform titles could be done more efficiently.
2. The AACR2 form of the name and uniform title was known from completing the authority work before searching for bibliographic records. Knowing the correct headings aided in searching OCLC, especially since bibliographic records may be inaccessible when using older forms of headings as search keys.

Disadvantages

1. With larger collections, pulling and sorting the shelflist cards by composer would be very time-consuming. This method will work well with smaller collections or within smaller ranges of class numbers.
2. The information on older cards is often incomplete and sometimes inaccurate. When authority work is based on information on the cards, the risk exists that the online bibliographic record may give fuller information. Authority work will then need to be repeated.
3. Bratcher recommended that student assistants be employed to retrieve publisher and plate numbers from items on the shelves. However, the author's experience with many older records on OCLC has shown that even when publisher or plate number information was present in the imprint field or a note field in the online record, it was not always entered in an 028 field. In this case, the time and effort of retrieving the information from the items would be wasted. The need for publisher or plate numbers as the sole means to identify matches occurs infrequently. Again, with a larger collection, this step would be impractical, if not impossible.

The Music Library at *Bowling Green State University*, a branch library housed within the main library, currently holds 9,950 scores. Retrospective conversion of the library's entire collection, begun in

1978 in the cataloging department, was managed by the department's head. Two part-time technical assistants were hired to work a total of forty hours per week. The recon assistants had no previous training in cataloging or in any of the special subject areas to be converted. Conversion of the music collection, approximately 4,000 scores and books, was completed by 1981.

Workflow

1. The assistant took a drawer from the shelflist and searched each non-OCLC generated card for matches. The definition of a match for purposes of recon tolerated slight differences in paging and size. Date could vary by one year and still be considered a match.
2. When a match was found, the assistant corrected any typographical errors, added local information, and updated the record.
3. Bibliographic information from cards with problems or with no match on OCLC was copied onto scrap cards and filed in a problem file, to be dealt with at the end of the recon project. Music problems were referred to the music librarian to resolve.
4. No authority work was performed. Authority problems were to be handled later in the local system, so that corrections could be made globally.

Advantages

1. Recon was completed relatively quickly and Bowling Green was able to implement their online system by the mid-1980s.
2. Even without a music background, the staff was able to successfully convert much of the music collection.

Disadvantages

1. Because of the complexities of music materials, incorrect records were often selected as matches. With no music background, the staff was unable to distinguish between similar

records. For example, bibliographic records for songs for high, medium, or low voice were not recognized as being bibliographically different. Many music titles had to be reconverted when it was discovered that the wrong online records had been used.

2. Because no authority work was done, the music records in the online system contained inaccurate or outdated name and title headings. Correction of these problems required the attention of several members of the professional staff.

The *Indiana University* Music Library is a branch library holding approximately 46,000 scores. The Music Library is an OCLC enhance library as well as a NACO music project participant, and the workflow was influenced by these factors. The staff consisted of one librarian, one full-time recon assistant, and thirty to forty hours per week of student assistants. In the four years of their participation in the AMLG recon project, Indiana converted over 36,000 score records.

Workflow

1. A student assistant examined the cards in the shelflist and marked cards as O (OCLC-generated) or W (withdrawn or missing), leaving those to be converted unmarked. At the same time, the cards in each category (OCLC, withdrawn, or to be converted) and in each class number were counted to provide an estimate of the number of titles to be converted.
2. Students searched OCLC for bibliographic and authority records.
2a. Early in the project, students also searched any headings not found in the LC authority file against the local authority file to find forms already used in the music library. This step usually provided no additional information. Since the manual catalogs were not to be corrected to reflect AACR2 changes, this step was discontinued. Headings were established regardless of those already existing in the card catalog, and no card maintenance was done for conflicting headings.

3. Records were not distributed according to level of cataloging difficulty, but all difficult records were converted by the librarian. Both the librarian and the recon assistant edited enhances and updates. However, the primary duty of the assistant was to proofread student inputting, complete OCLC transactions, and supervise the students.
4. Cards lacking OCLC matches were routed to the librarian, who made the decision to either completely recatalog the item or simply tag a photocopy of the card for input.
5. The librarian revised the assistant's editing and completed any difficult authority work.
6. Name headings not in the authority file were given to the librarian to establish, and to decide whether or not to submit to NACO. Uniform title headings not in the authority file were established by both the librarian and recon assistant. Titles perceived as frequently used or as creating searching problems on OCLC and which fell under LC guidelines for creating authority records were established by the librarian for submission to NACO.
7. Completed editing and new records were input into OCLC by students. Their work was printed and then saved online.
8. The recon assistant proofread all copy cataloging and the librarian proofread all new records.
9. Corrections were made online and the enhance and update transactions were completed by the recon assistant.
9a. With the implementation of the local online system, tape-loading was discontinued. The updated records were resaved and transferred into the local system by student assistants, who then added appropriate holdings information.
10. After a student refiled the shelflist cards, the filing was checked for accuracy by the recon assistant.

Advantages

1. Although the librarian or recon assistant could have searched for bibliographic records faster and more thoroughly than students could, the time to do so would have reduced avail-

able cataloging time. This was made evident when students were on break and the number of converted records dropped noticeably.

2. Converting the collection by class number saved time in that all pieces of one type, such as concertos or quartets, were converted at once. The staff became very familiar with the subject headings and rules for uniform titles for those types of compositions. It was not necessary to learn rules for new subject and uniform title headings with each record, as when converting the collection by composer.

3. The staff worked only with the shelflist and did not disrupt the public card catalog. Library users continued to have access to items being converted through the public catalog.

4. Since the recon assistant was trained to do both updates and enhances, fewer records were considered too difficult. This avoided an accumulation of the more difficult records to be completed by the librarian.

Disadvantages

1. Authority work for uniform titles was repeated every time a composer was encountered.

2. It was necessary on occasion, especially when converting choral music, to consult the main entry card in the public catalog for subject headings because neither the shelflist card nor the bibliographic record contained enough information to formulate a correct subject heading.

3. Training a library assistant to do all levels of music cataloging and then reviewing that work takes time. There may be a trade-off in the amount of time this takes and how much time it saves. Because of the grant project time limitations and staff turnover, only one month was allotted at Indiana for training each new recon assistant. Only so much cataloging can be taught in such a short training period.

4. The student assistants, untrained in cataloging rules, had to guess the AACR2 form of names and uniform titles in order to find authority records or pattern title headings, and in some cases even to search for bibliographic records. Often they

failed to find bibliographic or authority records because of their limited cataloging knowledge.
5. Temporary slips indicating that shelflist cards were pulled were not used because of the high number of cards removed from the shelflist. The danger of assigning a duplicate call number to a new item existed and did in fact occur.

The library at *Michigan State University* contracted with OCLC to convert all of its collection, including music. A total of 660,000 titles were converted at OCLC. Of the approximately 24,500 scores in Michigan State's collection, 11,000 needed conversion.

The music library is in the music building, where the scores (class M) and sound recordings are held. All books (ML) and all MTs are housed in the main library. The music cataloger works in the main library original cataloging unit. The shelflist is housed in the main library, with the music shelflist duplicated in the music library. Michigan State is an OCLC library with enhance status for scores; however, because of the workflow and the goal of completing recon quickly, recon records were not enhanced.

No extra personnel were hired for the recon project. However, music was the only area of recon consistently requiring a cataloger with subject specialization to resolve problems. OCLC assigned a specialist who worked with Michigan State throughout the entire project. They were fortunate in that this specialist had a background in music. No authority work was performed for records found on OCLC; the matching record was used as it appeared. Headings were later processed by a vendor. Analytics were added to records after they were loaded into the local system.

Workflow

1. Before recon was to begin, local specifications for the entire project were drafted. These were augmented for music, the only area in which the subject specialist expertise was required. In addition to guidelines for the general project, an additional eight pages of music-specific instructions were required regarding matching and choice of bibliographic record; format of score; and title, edition, imprint, and physi-

cal description areas, as well as concerns such as voice range and key. The library set up a priority order for sections of the shelflist to be converted. Music was converted last.

2. The shelflist itself was sent to OCLC, saving the time of photocopying each card. Thirty-five to seventy-five boxes of shelflist cards were shipped per week to OCLC, depending on the rate at which OCLC could convert the titles and return the cards. A numbering system was used to itemize the contents of each box and help locate any problems when the cards were returned.

3. While a section of the shelflist was at OCLC, temporary slips for newly-assigned call numbers were kept to be checked after that section was converted and returned.

4. OCLC staff searched for the matching record and added local information as requested in the specifications.

5. Problems were flagged by color to denote their nature. Cyrillic records needing transliteration, very old shelflist "temp slips," multiple matching OCLC records, or any records with areas of uncertainty were sent back unconverted.

6. All original records, except those identified as problems, were input at OCLC. Their staff searched the authority file for name and title headings for the new records. When headings were not found in the authority file, those on Michigan State's cards were used. Additionally, subject headings were used as they appeared on the cards.

7. Cards were converted and returned usually within six weeks.

8. Less than two months after OCLC began converting music titles, the music cataloger started receiving problem cards. Approximately 350 music cards were returned as problems. Among the problems were:

   a. format differences
   b. collation differences (a difference of 5 pages was allowed for music)
   c. size differences of more than 4 cm.
   d. variations in title

9. The music cataloger could choose to convert the problem records locally or return the cards to OCLC for conversion.

10. A student checked the returned cards for duplicate call numbers and for missing cards. Michigan State reported very few problems of either kind.

Both the music cataloger and the head of catalog management expressed satisfaction with the manner and speed with which OCLC converted their collection. Most problems seemed minor in the face of converting over 660,000 titles. Mary Black-Shier, the music cataloger, reports that the music conversion was handled in an efficient and timely manner.

Advantages

1. The collection was converted and loaded in the local database within a short amount of time, more quickly than if the local staff had had to search OCLC and input information themselves.
2. Recon could be completed without hiring extra staff.
3. Since OCLC had assigned a staff specialist with music knowledge to work on the project, problems which otherwise might have been missed were recognized and resolved.

Disadvantages

1. Michigan State relied on an outside agency for verification of headings in records converted by OCLC. The headings could be checked for accuracy of form, but not for accuracy of content.
2. The music cataloger had less control over content of the records than if they had been converted in-house.
3. Even though no new personnel were hired, the music cataloger's time was required for resolution of problems OCLC had returned.

The Music Library at the *University of California-Berkeley* has completed its conversion of approximately 45,000 scores,[13] funded in part by the Title II-C and RLG grants. For the pilot year of the AMLG project, UC-Berkeley used RLIN for conversion. In the first and second years of the project, they sent photocopies of their shelflist cards to OCLC for conversion. By the second full year, UC-Berkeley had use of a functioning local system. At this time, their staff consisted of three levels of part-time recon assistants: library assistant II, III, and IV. The latter functioned as manager and supervisor of the recon project.

Workflow

1. Guidelines for OCLC were drawn up via negotiations between the head of technical services in the music library and OCLC.
2. All cards to be converted were pulled, photocopied, cut into card-sized slips, and mailed to OCLC to be searched and converted.
3. OCLC staff added only call number and holdings information to the matching records. No other changes were made.
4. The slips were mailed back from OCLC, the material having been converted according to UC-Berkeley's guidelines, or marked as not found or as a problem of some sort. The slips were separated into two categories: converted and not converted.
5. The OCLC-converted records were tape-loaded into the local system and then checked by the library assistant II, who verified both bibliographic and holdings information for accuracy. At this stage, data in the fixed field and 04X fields were added or corrected.
6. With each tape-load, the local system printed lists of all headings on the tape: name, name/uniform title, series, and subject headings. The headings were searched against the LC authority file by the library assistant II, who then made corrections to the records. The library assistant IV, responsible for authority work on all of the headings not found in the authority file, used the system's capacity for global changes for maintenance.
7. The library assistant III searched the records not converted by OCLC in RLIN and converted them on RLIN when matches were found. Records with no match in either database were input into the local system. All new records and authority

work were revised by the library assistant IV. Problems which could not be resolved at this level were referred to the music library's head of technical services.

Advantages

1. As a result of preparing the cards all at once for OCLC, a clear picture emerged of what and how much had to be converted.
2. The time to do the first bibliographic search was saved.[14]
3. The strengths of the online system could be used for the authority work on the tape-loaded records.
4. The work was immediately available in the database and completely fixable in case of error.
5. It was possible to hire people at varying level of skills, easing the problems of training and revision.

Disadvantages

1. The library assistant IV questioned how much time had actually been saved by contracting OCLC to convert the records, considering the time it took to prepare, send, and receive records from OCLC and the number of times it was necessary to access the OCLC-converted records.
2. In contrast to the pilot year, when RLIN was used, it was necessary to return to the converted records frequently for corrections.
3. Since it was necessary to return frequently to the bibliographic records for authority work, making the printout of all the headings and then working from that printout may have created more trouble than it saved.
4. In the pilot year of the recon project, all staff members worked on an equal level. This produced a more collegial environment with better exchange of information and mutual problem-solving, than when different levels of staff were assigned different levels of work.
5. It might have been more efficient to have all the staff trained at the same level so that each record was dealt with once, by

one person, rather than being divided into pieces and handled by several levels of personnel.

The Eda Kuhn Loeb Music Library at *Harvard* is a branch library housed in the music department. The collection is classified in part on an alphabetical arrangement by composer. Of a total of 60,000 scores, approximately 58,000 needed to be converted. In the first year of the AMLG recon project, Harvard converted works by the "big 18" composers, selected on the basis of the strengths of their collection. In the following years they have converted the remainder of their collection alphabetically, working on RLIN. The staff consisted of one librarian, two part-time library assistants, and thirty hours per week of student assistants.

Workflow

1. An experienced student pulled the main entry cards for scores from the public card catalog. Since this could be complicated, the process was monitored by the librarian, who reviewed all the cards selected for recon. Drawers with cards removed were marked to notify users.
2. Students searched for bibliographic records on RLIN.
3. A library assistant organized the results in batches and searched the authority file for all name and title records.
4. The bibliographic and authority records were distributed to the staff for editing. The librarian converted the difficult items, but otherwise all similar records were kept together to avoid duplication of authority work. No distinction was made between records with matches and new records because, as on OCLC, creating a new record could often be easier than upgrading an existing record. Therefore, all levels of staff did all levels of cataloging.
5. The librarian reviewed the staff's work and did the research necessary to establish name and title headings for which no authority records were available. Library assistants who were interested in doing authority work for names and uniform titles were encouraged to do so; however, their work was

revised by the librarian, since the responsibility for authority work was hers.

6. Students input changes and new records and printed out their work.
7. All staff proofread the inputting.
8. The students input corrections and completed the transaction.
9. Cards for converted items were refiled in the main card catalog.
10. When the RLIN tape was loaded onto the local system, a library assistant checked headings known to be on that tape, looking for reversed digits in dates and commonly misspelled words (e.g., paino, scared choruses, Mozrat, etc.)

Advantages

1. Converting by composer maximized the use of online authority searching and offline authority work. Not only did composer remain the same from card to card, but frequently so did editor, librettist, and series.
2. Harvard's main entry cards contained fuller information than found on the shelflist card.

Disadvantages

1. An aggravating amount of time was spent on records for items little in demand while composers at the end of the alphabet, Verdi, for example, waited to be converted.
2. It may have been more advantageous to proceed from the shelflist and omit pulling cards from the main catalog and inconveniencing the library users.
3. Perhaps more effort than is worthwhile was required to pull and then refile cards which, after integration in an online catalog, would become superfluous. Shelflist cards will still be of use, even after conversion.

The *Cornell University* Music Library holds approximately 50,000 scores, of which an estimated 20,400 needed conversion. The music library is a branch library with its own shelflist, which is duplicated in the central technical services unit. Music recon was done in the main library, away from the music collection. The music library shelflist was used as source of information because the holdings information was more accurate than that in the shelflist in the central technical services unit. The staff consisted of one full time librarian, two part-time senior recon assistants, and one student assistant who worked eight hours per week. Other students were used as needed.

Workflow

1. Cards to be converted were pulled from the music library shelflist, and photocopied by the student assistant. The corresponding cards in the main library shelflist were stamped to denote that those cards had been converted.
2. The student then checked the public catalog in the main library for any missing tracings and annotated the shelflist card photocopy. The recon assistants completed this step when RLIN was down. The headings on the shelflist card were then used as the basis for authority work, rather than the headings found in the matching RLIN records.
3. The recon assistants searched the authority file on RLIN for the headings found on the shelflist card.
4. All name, uniform title, and series headings were established by the librarian, working from printouts of authority file records. When a heading was not found in the authority file, the local system was checked. If the heading was found there, that form was used so that the local system was consistent. When name headings were not found in either, the librarian searched for predominant usage on RLIN. All subject headings were reviewed and brought up to LCSH standards by the librarian.
5. After the authority work was completed, the recon assistants searched RLIN for bibliographic records.
6. All editing and inputting for matches was done at the terminal by the recon assistants. Changes and additional headings were input as noted by the librarian on the photocopies of the cards. During their initial training period, which lasted one

year, the librarian revised the recon assistants' work and completed the RLIN transactions. When the training period was over and the librarian felt their work was sufficiently accurate, their work was not revised.

7. When a heading appeared in an RLIN record which had not been found in the public catalog, the librarian was consulted for appropriateness and form of heading. This occurred only occasionally and caused little disruption to the workflow.

8. New records were tagged and input directly into RLIN by the recon assistants.

9. Cyrillic records were converted by the librarian. Any CJK or Hebrew records were routed to the respective original catalogers to convert.

Advantages

1. The idiosyncracies of uniform titles and subject headings in a particular class number range were learned and reinforced more easily by converting in call number order from the shelflist.

2. Because the public catalog was checked for headings, authority work could be completed before going to the utility. This made it possible for lower-level staff to edit records online and saved the librarian the step of proofreading every record once it was input.

Disadvantages

1. Converting records in call number order made the authority work much more labor-intensive.

2. Converting scores in the cataloging department, rather than in the Music Library, did not cause many problems, although at times the librarian felt frustrated at being removed from the scores for the authority work. It was sometimes necessary to call the music library or to take over an accumulation of questions concerning holdings or authority work. Occasionally

they had to rely on the RLIN record to answer some questions, such as language of vocal works.

CONCLUSION

These seven libraries provide a cross-section of differently sized libraries with differently oriented collections and different approaches to retrospective conversion. Because score recon is an expensive and time-demanding venture, each library sought to use to potential the staff and workflow within their time and budgetary limitations. The AMLG and RLG libraries received external funding and were able to do extensive authority work and conversion bordering on recataloging. Their goal was to benefit the entire music library community. The smaller libraries, under stricter budget constraints, could not be expected to make such an investment. All seven libraries attempted to control the high cost of score recon by carefully planning the method, workflow, and level of staffing. Even after the recon process was in place, however, adjustments were made to restructure or eliminate procedures that were inefficient or unnecessary.

The location of tracings, subject headings, and holdings information, on the shelflist or the main entry card, will influence the choice of source of cataloging information. In either case, the online bibliographic record usually includes enough information to convert regardless of age or brevity of cataloging on the card. It would be necessary to have complete information on the card only when authority work is done before searching for the bibliographic record, as Cornell and Northern Kentucky did. However, Cornell found it necessary to search each shelflist card in the public catalog, where more complete information was found. Because shelflist cards at Indiana were frequently incomplete, the staff relied on the online record for additional information or consulted the public catalog. The former can be risky and the latter was disruptive to the workflow. Harvard used the main entry card as the source of cataloging information because the music shelflist cards did not include subject headings or notes. In some cases, so little information existed that the shelflist card functioned as little more than a "place-holder." They found that the average amount of time cards were out of the public catalog was thirty days. The location of the cards during that time was noted on the drawer from which they were pulled, and on occasion, users were referred to technical services to access the cards. While it is important to consider the extent of cataloging information on the shelflist or main entry card, the consequences of either choice on the rest of the library should also be assessed. Pulling cards from the public catalog would make those items inaccessible to the user through the main entry. Removing cards from the shelflist increases the possibility of assigning duplicate call numbers. In either case, time must be spent pulling, refiling, and dropping cards.

The choice of cataloging information will also have an impact on authority work. Working from main entry cards or batching shelflist cards by composer avoids repetition of authority work when establishing uniform titles. The trade-off is the familiarity of uniform title rules and subject heading practice gained when converting by class. In the pilot year of the AMLG recon project, Indiana combined the best of these two possibilities: shelflist cards within categories of LC class M40 to the M500s were arranged by composer, significantly speeding authority work. This worked well because a high number of composers were repeated within a small range of class numbers.[15]

The order in which music scores are to be converted is a decision to be made on two levels: when will music be converted in relation to the library collection as a whole, and in what order will the scores be converted within class M. The former is frequently decided at a higher level and the decision can often be out of the hands of the music librarian. Tim Cherubini's discussion of music recon covers this aspect well. The latter can be decided in the planning stages of score recon. The most obvious approach is to begin at M1 and convert to the end of the MTs. It might be advisable to begin with less problematic sections of class M (organ and piano music, for example) to provide an initial sense of accomplishment and speed. Other approaches are to begin in areas of high demand or to target collection strengths.

Level of staffing is an important issue in score conversion, and will affect everything from cost of recon to workflow. The seven libraries profiled above exhibit a wide range of staffing levels. Student assistants were used at the risk of their inexperience in both the subject of music and in library practices. Bowling Green and Northern Kentucky used no student assistants. UC-Berkeley, Cornell, and Michigan State used students for preliminary work such as pulling cards, photocopying, or checking the card catalog for tracings. Harvard used students to input edited and new records into RLIN, while Indiana relied on students for even higher level tasks such as searching for bibliographic and authority records. The risks involved in using student assistants for higher level tasks must be weighed against the amount of time that would then be available to higher levels of staff for other conversion tasks.

Use of library assistants also varied widely. Score recon at Northern Kentucky was done entirely by the librarian, with no paraprofessional involvement. With the exception of Michigan State, the other libraries made heavy use of paraprofessional staff for all or most of the recon process. The larger libraries found it inefficient to distribute records according to level of cataloging difficulty, with the exception of the most difficult records. Paraprofessional staff at three of the libraries, UC-Berkeley, Cornell, and Harvard, were in fact responsible for creating new records. Using the paraprofessional staff in this capacity helped to create a collegial atmosphere, eliminated steps in the decision making process, and reduced the number of times a record was handled. Additionally, the librarians were able to use more of their time performing difficult authority work and conversion, training staff, and writing manuals. The trade-off is that heavy paraprofessional involvement requires an extensive training and revision period when time is already limited. When staff turnover is high, as it was with several of these libraries, repeated training periods can reduce productivity of the recon project.

Authority work was done by varying levels of staff. At Cornell and Northern Kentucky, it was limited to the professional level. The librarian at Cornell felt that music uniform titles are too complex for temporary staff to learn to establish with a high degree of accuracy. Their workflow was organized around the foundation of having all authority work completed by the librarian before the library assistants searched for online records, thus eliminating the time-consuming step of revision. At UC-Berkeley, Harvard, and Indiana, library assistants did some or all of the authority work. At Indiana, the training and revision for this was an on-going process, demanding more of the librarian's attention each time conversion in a new section of the shelflist was begun. The library assistants at Harvard were able to do about fifty percent of all authority work. However, the librarian pointed out that the remaining fifty percent was on a more difficult level and required more of her time than was required to complete the easier authority work. And although fifty percent of the authority work could be done at the paraprofessional level, it was necessary for the librarian to review *all* the authority work.

UC-Berkeley and Michigan State both found contracting recon to OCLC to be a viable alternative to in-house conversion. Scores were converted very quickly and the records were available online very soon after conversion. However, the need for staff involvement was not eliminated, nor did it eliminate the need for music expertise. The steps of identifying and photocopying the cards to be converted, packing and shipping them to OCLC, and sorting them upon return still existed. Michigan State found that bypassing the first step of pulling and photocopying cards resulted in no major problems. OCLC converted all of Michigan State's records, those with copy as well as new records. Additionally, OCLC staff searched all headings in the authority file and made corrections to the bibliographic records. As a result, even less involvement was necessary from the music cataloger. UC-Berkeley chose to examine the OCLC-converted records for accuracy and verify all headings once the records were tape-loaded into the local system, as well as to convert locally the items with no copy. These decisions necessitated a very different workflow and level of staffing than required at Michigan State.

While speed is gained by contracting to a utility, some control over the content of the converted record is lost. Even when specific guidelines are drawn up for the utility, local practices in note fields and other areas will be missed. The music cataloger at Michigan

State acknowledged that there was additional information that she would have preferred to see in the converted records. The recon staff at UC-Berkeley found it necessary to access the records several times to make changes and additions to them. In both cases, the librarians involved stressed the importance of developing very specific guidelines for OCLC to follow, owing to the complex nature of searching music materials and identifying matches.

Since one of the goals of retrospective conversion is the creation of a local automated database, name, uniform title, series, and subject headings must be brought under control at some point in the conversion process. The size and goal of the project both affect the time at which the authority work is done. The smaller libraries chose to get the bibliographic records into the local system as quickly and inexpensively as possible, without changing the national database. Music authority work could be performed by a vendor or by staff on the local system. The larger libraries, all involved in national projects, had as one of their goals to increase and enhance music coverage in the national databases. Thus, authority work was performed on the online bibliographic record, according to strict guidelines. Tucker commented on the extremely high cost of creating *"the* national record upon which other institutions can base their conversion activities."[16] All the AMLG libraries experienced the conflict of fulfilling this goal while meeting local needs. While Tucker wondered if "cheaper alternatives" exist, Crismond reported that the majority of libraries responding in a survey favored maintaining high standards in all conversion projects and expressed a "strong concern for the quality of the database, [and] a desire not to repeat the past mistakes of minimal records, [giving] a greater weighting toward future uses of the database . . ."[17]

The problems associated with music authority work and the formulation of subject headings are compounded when dealing with old or incomplete cataloging. Staff with music knowledge may have less difficulty with uniform titles since the concept of generic and distinctive titles would be easily understood. However, learning the complexities of uniform titles can be challenging even with a music background. Underlying Tucker's statement that "one no longer talks so much of 'establishing' a music uniform title, but rather of 'researching' it"[18] is the need for staff with musicological background and knowledge of reference sources and research methods, in addition to familiarity with AACR2. As Donna Lester, the music retrospective conversion librarian at Cornell states, authority work in music recon projects is quite overwhelming and not thoroughly thought through by administrators planning for recon.

All of these factors–source of cataloging information, what to convert, in what order to convert, and the level of staffing, as well as the issue of when and how to do authority work–combined together to determine the workflows of the score recon projects profiled above. The special needs of score recon required careful pre-recon planning, a judicious use of staff, and a honing of workflow.

NOTES

1. Maureen D. Finn, "How to Prepare for Retrospective Conversion, *Bulletin of the American Society for Information Science* 13, no. 4 (April/May, 1987): 23.

2. Five articles deal specifically with retrospective conversion of music materials: Perry Bratcher, "Music OCLC Recon: The Practical Approach," *Cataloging & Classification Quarterly* 8, no. 2 (1987/88): 41-48; Tim Cherubini, "Retrospective Conversion and the Music Librarian," *MOUG Newsletter* 48 (August 1991): 10-12; Vivian Olsen, "Three Research Libraries Convert Music Materials," *Research Libraries in OCLC* 23 (1987): 1-7; Ruth W. Tucker, "Music Retrospective Conversion at the University of California Berkeley," *Technical Services Quarterly* 7, no. 2 (1989): 13-28; and Richard B. Wursten and James S. Chervinko, "Music Goes On-line: Retrospective Conversion of Card Catalog Records for Music Scores at Morris Library (SIU-C)," *Illinois Libraries* 65 (May 1983): 346-348.

3. Sara C. Heitshu and Joan H. Quinn, "Serials Conversion at the University of Michigan," *Drexel Library Quarterly* 21, no. 1 (Winter 1985): 64.

4. Michael D. DiCarlo and Margaret W. Maxfield, "Sequential Analysis as a Sampling Test for Inventory Need," *The Journal of Academic Librarianship* 13, no. 6 (January 1988): 345.

5. Karla D. Peterson, "Planning for Serials Retrospective Conversion," *Serials Review* 10, no. 3 (Fall 1984): 74.

6. AMLG membership comprises ten major research music libraries at Cornell University, Eastman School of Music, Harvard University, Indiana University, Stanford University, University of California-Berkeley, Yale University, University of California-Los Angeles, University of Illinois, and University of Michigan. All but the last three have participated in the score recon project, which began with a pilot year in 1985-1986. The project resumed in 1987 and is now in its

fifth year of funding. Two libraries involved in the project, UC-Berkeley and Indiana, have completed score recon and begun sound recording conversion.

7. As of March 31, 1991, 172,573 score records had been converted, of which 72% were significantly enhanced or new to either RLIN or OCLC.

8. The NACO (Name Authority Cooperative) Music Project, coordinated at Indiana University, has as its goal to correct the under-representation of music headings in the LC authority file. The project began in 1987 with Indiana and Eastman, and has expanded to include all AMLG grant libraries as well as other music libraries.

9. Tucker, "Retrospective Conversion," 15.

10. Peterson, "Planning for Serials Retrospective Conversion," 73.

11. Jack Krantz, "Paraprofessional Involvement in Music Cataloging: A Case Study," *Cataloging & Classification Quarterly* 10, no. 4 (1990): 89-98.

12. The OCLC enhance program began in 1984. Selected libraries have the ability to modify or add to "master" records, in effect functioning in a quality control capacity and eliminating the need for every library to make the same corrections each time a record is used.

13. Tucker, "Retrospective Conversion," 15-16.

14. Tucker, "Retrospective Conversion," 20. OCLC had estimated, based on a sample, that it would take three months just to search for the 10,000 score bibliographic records.

15. Olsen, "Three Research Libraries," 4.

16. Tucker, "Retrospective Conversion," 16.

17. Linda F. Crismond, "Quality Issues in Retrospective Conversion Projects," *Library Resources and Technical Services* 25 (January 1981): 51.

18. Tucker, "Retrospective Conversion," 17.

BIBLIOGRAPHY

Bratcher, Perry. "Music OCLC Recon: The Practical Approach." *Cataloging & Classification Quarterly* 8, no. 2 (1987/88): 41-48.

Cherubini, Tim. "Retrospective Conversion and the Music Librarian." *MOUG Newsletter* 48 (August 1991): 10-12.

Collins, Jane D. "Planning for Retrospective Conversion." *Art Documentation* 1, no. 3/4 (Summer 1982): 92-94.

Crismond, Linda F. "Quality Issues in Retrospective Conversion Projects." *Library Resources and Technical Services* 25 (January 1981): 48-55.

DiCarlo, Michael D., and Margaret W. Maxfield. "Sequential Analysis as a Sampling Test for Inventory Need." *The Journal of Academic Librarianship* 13, no. 6 (January 1988): 345-348.

Finn, Maureen D. "How to Prepare for Retrospective Conversion." *Bulletin of the American Society for Information Science* 13, no. 4 (April/May 1987): 23-24.

Heitshu, Sara C., and Joan H. Quinn. "Serials Conversion at the University of Michigan." *Drexel Library Quarterly* 21, no. 1 (Winter 1985): 62-76.

Krantz, Jack. "Paraprofessional Involvement in Music Cataloging: A Case Study" *Cataloging & Classification Quarterly* 10, no. 4 (1990): 89-98.

Olsen, Vivian. "Three Research Libraries Convert Music Materials." *Research Libraries in OCLC* 23 (1987): 1-7.

Peterson, Karla D. "Planning for Serials Retrospective Conversion." *Serials Review* 10, no. 3 (Fall 1984): 73-78.

Ryans, Cynthia C., and Margaret F. Soule, "Preparations for Retrospective Conversion: An Empirical Study." *Catholic Library World* 55 (December 1983): 221-223.

Tucker, Ruth W. "Music Retrospective Conversion at the University of California at Berkeley." *Technical Services Quarterly* 7, no. 2 (1989): 13-28.

Wursten, Richard B., and James S. Chervinko. "Music Goes On-line: Retrospective Conversion of Card Catalog Records for Music Scores at Morris Library (SIU-C)." *Illinois Libraries* 65 (May 1983): 346-348.

Streamlining a Conversion Project with a Staff PC Workstation and Shelf List Sampling

Beth Sandore

SUMMARY. Several novel methods used at the University of Illinois at Urbana/Champaign to enable more efficient retrospective conversion projects are explored in this paper. First, a staff PC workstation interface was developed to facilitate processing of shelf list information, both for the local online catalog and for OCLC cataloging. Second, shelf list sampling was used to derive cost estimates for the project. Recommendations for future use of these and similar methods are discussed.

INTRODUCTION

The prospect of converting catalog cards into electronic form is at once both exhilarating and exhausting. It is exhilarating because the end-result enables increased access to materials that were previously available only through a card catalog. However, the exhaustion sets in with the realization that this process requires countless hours of painstakingly careful human scrutiny, in spite of the substantial cost for electronic upgrades of obsolete headings, and as-

Beth Sandore is Assistant Automated Services Librarian and Assistant Professor of Library Administration at the University of Illinois at Urbana/Champaign Library.

The author gratefully acknowledges the contributions of the members of the planning team for this project: Winnie Chan and Doris Osterbur, Automated Services; William Mischo, Engineering Library; William Kubitz, Zigrida Arbatsky, and Ruth Aydt, Computer Science Department; and, the assistance of Mary Ellen Farrell, now of the Illinois Library Computer Systems Office.

sorted other projects to remove duplicate records, or to untangle and reconcile other resultant problems.

It was with well-tempered exhilaration that a data conversion process was undertaken recently at the University of Illinois at Urbana-Champaign Library, in conjunction with the University's Department of Computer Science. This paper describes several innovative methods used to simplify the data conversion, re-cataloging, and the associated technical services workflow. These methods contributed to effective completion of this project. The particularly noteworthy method used in this project was the development of a PC interface program to create a staff processing workstation. This program was developed to enable quick initial searching, sorting, and entry of manual card file information for the Library's local online catalog and for later OCLC searching. Another novel method employed was the use of random sampling of the monograph portion of the holdings to form the basis for cost and labor analysis. Next, the Library adopted the approach of integrating the conversion into its regular staffing workflow. Finally, detailed descriptions of the technical services workflow used in this project are provided.

THE DEPARTMENT OF COMPUTER SCIENCE: AN ISOLATED DATA CONVERSION PROJECT

Like other research libraries around the country, the University of Illinois is active in bringing together and organizing access to bibliographic resources in electronic format. One example of this activity was demonstrated in the effort to provide access to the Computer Science reading room collection through the Library's online catalog. Although the Computer Science departmental reading room collection was sizeable–approximately 8,000 titles and 15,000 volumes–it was not yet electronically accessible. Both faculty and students in the department saw distinct advantages to combining their collection electronically with the University Library's collections. Computer scientists wished to have easy access to an electronic database of their own holdings and those of the campus library system. The added statewide resource-sharing dimension to this catalog was further incentive for this collaborative effort.

This system is also a statewide online catalog for over 800 libraries in Illinois, based at the University of Illinois (UIUC). At the UIUC Library, ILLINET Online provides author, subject, keyword title, and many other search capabilities for searching over 1.5 million titles, as well as circulation, call number, holdings, and location information for over 3 million titles in a collection of over 7 million volumes. The Library and University community, recognizing the strength in the curriculum, believed the inclusion of the Computer Science holdings would be of benefit to both the campus and the broader state community. With these goals in mind, the Library developed a plan for expediting this project.

PLANNING

The key activities in this project included: (1) coordinating the re-cataloging and retrospective conversion (in the Library's centrally located technical processing unit–Automated Services); and (2) setting into place ongoing procedures for Library processing of Computer Science materials which were currently received. The author, working with a coordinating team, was responsible for the project. The coordinating team comprised three staff members from Automated Services, a departmental liaison from the Engineering Library, and three staff members from the Computer Science Department, including a programmer. The expertise in the group included considerable experience in PC programming for technical services applications, knowledge of cataloging and processing workflow, and familiarity with the scope and nature of materials in the Computer Science collection.

After several fruitful planning sessions the project team developed a plan. The guidelines for the project are listed in priority order:

1. Estimate the cost of the shelf list processing for each aspect of the project (staff, OCLC searching and inputting, and computer equipment);

2. Do as much preliminary automatic processing as possible, thereby integrating the materials quickly into the normal workflow of the unit;
3. Find the best way to make the preliminary processing simple enough for student workers to perform;
4. Determine how best to use regular staff (professional, para-professional, support, and student) already trained and skilled in OCLC searching, inputting, copy, and original cataloging;
5. Design the plan for integrating the ongoing Computer Science processing (cataloging, marking, and binding) into current procedures as closely as possible.

ONLINE TECHNICAL PROCESSING ENVIRONMENT

Before the details of this project are discussed, a brief description of the online catalog and the technical processing environment at the UIUC Library may be helpful. The cataloging and database maintenance workflow at UIUC can best be depicted in a continuous flow (see Figure 1–"Technical Processing Workflow: Automated Services".) With the exception of a few units (the Slavic, Map & Geography, Music, and Asian libraries) the production part of cataloging (OCLC searching and inputting, and copy cataloging) is centralized in the Automated Services unit. Original cataloging of serials is completed by a small centralized unit. At this time, original cataloging of monographs is done in a decentralized fashion by departmental librarians; however, after some internal evaluation in 1989, this arrangement is slated to change to something on the order of a small centralized original cataloging unit in the future. After completed copy slips have been reviewed, they are returned to Automated Services and are input into OCLC by staff in Automated Services. Clark and Chan (1985) provide a more detailed description of the cataloging, inputting, and database maintenance workflow.

OCLC is now used for all cataloging in the Library. Much of the collection is classed according to the Dewey Decimal classification scheme. The database for the Library's online catalog–ILLINET Online–is constructed from the cataloging and local information

FIGURE 1. Technical Processing Workflow: Automated Services*

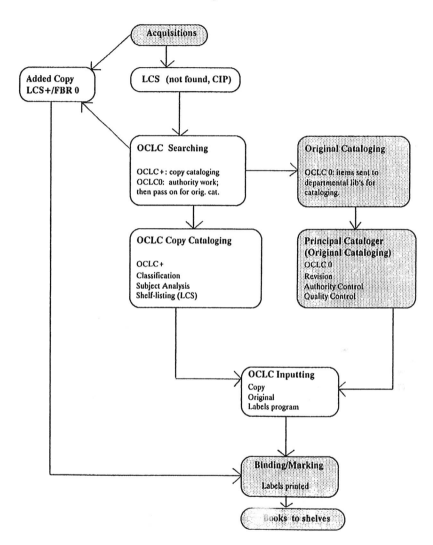

*Shaded areas represent processing done outside of Automated Services. (University of Illinois Library/Urbana 2/91)

which is input into OCLC (see Figure 2–"How Information Enters ILLINET Online".) Local data such as location, holdings, and volume and copy numbers, are entered into the 049 field of the OCLC record at the time of cataloging. The Illinois State Library purchases the OCLC archival tape for the 800 OCLC/ILLINET libraries in the state, including UIUC. The holdings information, along with the call number, author, title, place, and date of publication, is stripped from the OCLC archival record to form the circulation record in LCS (Library Computer System)–the Library's circulation database. Bibliographic descriptions and headings are stripped from the OCLC archival record to create FBR (Full Bibliographic Record)–the bibliographic component of ILLINET Online, a Western Library Network software product (see Figure 3–"LCS and FBR File Structures".) This information is stripped on a weekly basis through "grinder" programs created by the administrative computing center (AISS), whose programming and technical staff support the ILLINET Online database in cooperation with the Library and the remaining statewide network, ILCSO (Illinois Library Computer Systems Organization) (Salika, 1985).

Although the LCS and FBR databases are separate, the LCS circulation information is linked to its corresponding FBR bibliographic information through a link file which is rebuilt each week after the OCLC archival tapes are processed. Once the records have entered the ILLINET Online database, necessary maintenance performed is as follows:

LCS

1. Batch mode: SUPERWYLBUR–using a somewhat antiquated, yet still functional mainframe line-mode editor; referred to as SWYL, the editor is used by the Automated Records Maintenance unit to perform a high volume of major changes to the LCS record (adding copies to existing titles, changing library location codes and loan periods en masse, and correcting typographical errors;) SWYL files are processed once a week; a number of PC programs have been developed by Prof. Winnie Chan, Head of Automated Records Maintenance, to

provide a simple, interactive link with SUPERWYLBUR for Library staff who perform maintenance;

OR

2. Real-time: Workfile–a basic editing program in LCS, which is used for minor changes to call numbers, locations, and loan periods; Workfile is used mainly by individual departmental library staff to perform simple, low-volume maintenance on their own LCS monograph holdings.

FBR

1. Batch mode, full-screen editor: FBR online authority work and database maintenance can be performed using an FBR full-screen editing program–Input/Edit–which is a module within the FBR software. FBR online authority work involves adding, deleting, or merging headings in an online, Library of Congress-based authority file. Online bibliographic editing in FBR involves the correction of coding and tagging errors, the addition of notes, and the correction of typographical errors.

LCS SUPERWYLBUR files are processed in batch mode once a week; FBR database maintenance and authority work is processed and added to the database in daily batch mode. Adding or deleting a library holdings symbol from FBR is done through OCLC, as is copy cataloging and inputting of original cataloging records. Online authority control and database maintenance using FBR has changed somewhat since the completion of the Computer Science project; it now encompasses a statewide consortium. In a recent article, Henigman (1991) describes the development of this statewide cooperative online authority control system.

Close attention to cataloging detail was important because of the complexity of the online environment and the necessity of re-cataloging this collection. For instance, added copies might fall into one of two processing categories: (1) a "true" added copy, where both an LCS and an FBR record for the item indicated on the shelf list

FIGURE 2. How Information Enters ILLINET Online*

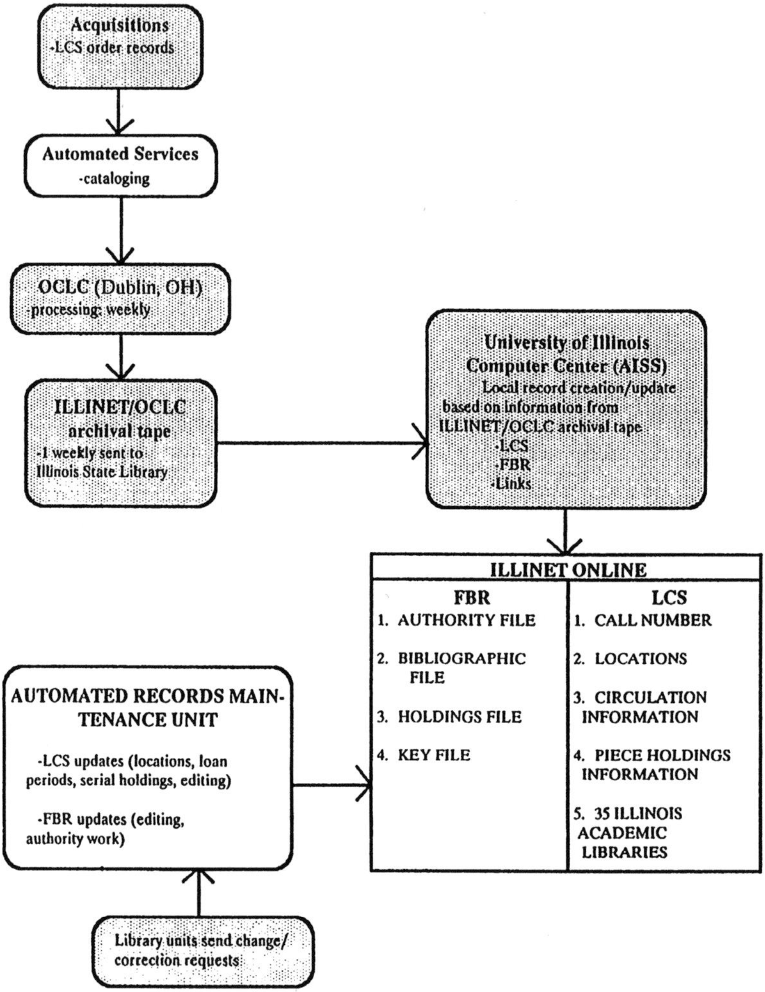

*Shaded areas represent processing done outside of Automated Services. (University of Illinois Library/Urbana 2/91)

card already existed in the database. These were simply added through SUPERWYLBUR; (2) a "half" added copy, where the item had been cataloged and classed (pre-OCLC) with an LCS brief circulation and call number record, but no FBR bibliographic record. Alternatively, since the UIUC Library shared a bibliographic database at the time with the River Bend Library System, the FBR record might appear in our database, but closer examination would reveal that it was in fact cataloged on OCLC by River Bend, and held only by River Bend, with no link to our LCS circulation file. These items required updating through OCLC. This process adds the UIUC holdings symbol to OCLC, and, by virtue of the local automatic programs, strips the OCLC record from the archival tape, adds it to FBR, creates a link to the corresponding LCS record, and adds the new copy and location information to LCS. As was already mentioned, copy and original cataloging through OCLC create both LCS and FBR records automatically in the ILLINET On-

FIGURE 3. LCS & FBR File Structures

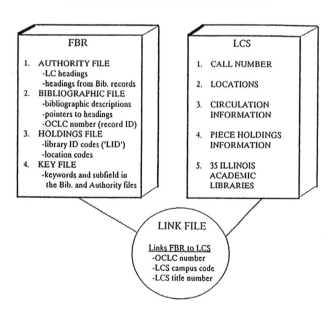

line database. With all of these complex processing capabilities, it was necessary to obtain an estimate of what type and how much processing could be anticipated.

SAMPLING THE COLLECTION

In order to determine how many of the estimated 8,000 titles in the Computer Science collection were monographs, serials, or proceedings, a random sample of the shelf list was drawn. The existing shelf list in the Computer Science Library was physically divided into three parts–monographs, proceedings, and serials. Each portion was treated separately in the sampling process. A 10% random sample was taken from each shelf list in order to estimate what type of processing might be needed to put the holdings into LCS and to allow subject access through FBR, to determine which Library staff would be involved, and to project what costs would be incurred.

Although samples were taken from each of the three shelf lists, this paper focuses on the monograph processing for the project. The percentage of monographs in the collection was by far the greatest–88% of the collection. Only monographs were arranged in a classified order on the shelves. The classification scheme in use was an in-house, broad subject system, developed by the Computer Science Department. In essence, the collection needed to be recataloged using the Dewey Decimal classification scheme and LC name and subject headings. Cataloging the monographs first was of primary importance, as the collection had to be physically re-arranged in Dewey call number order once the conversion was complete. With an online shelf list in LCS, there was no need for the Computer Science paper shelf list to be re-organized according to Dewey, as it would eventually be phased out. The straightforward nature of monograph processing also lent itself nicely to exploring PC workstation applications for processing the shelf list.

With these considerations in mind, a 10% random sample was drawn from the monograph shelf list of approximately 7,000 titles. These 655 titles were searched to determine what type of processing each would require. In order to avoid the bias toward selecting thick shelf list cards over thin cards, the Fussler technique was used. This sampling technique involves measuring and flagging equal intervals throughout the shelf list, then selecting the third card behind the interval boundary (Fussler, 1969). In later research on card file sampling, Bookstein reinforces the potential accuracy in the use of this technique, but cautions samplers about other less obvious problems that can skew a sample (Bookstein, 1983).

The collection was divided into three categories of materials, according to the type of processing needed: (1) *added copies* to the online system (with both a circulation and a bibliographic record in LCS and FBR); (2) books that required *copy cataloging* (in LCS *or* FBR; and found in OCLC); and (3) items requiring *original cataloging* (not in LCS or FBR; not found in OCLC). The results of the sample (see Table 1) indicated that over half of the titles would be added copy, therefore requiring the least amount of processing. The sample results also suggested that slightly less than half of the titles in the monograph collection would require copy cataloging, with a small percentage needing original cataloging.

Table 2 reveals the actual processing figures which were tallied at the finish of the project. A comparison of the figures indicates that the error rate for the sample is not within the normal 95% confidence interval in the case of added copies. There are two causes for this inaccuracy. One explanation is the fact that the sample size does not accurately represent the population. The actual num-

TABLE 1. Monograph Shelf List Sample. Total = 7,000 {approx.} titles, N = 655 titles

	ADDED COPIES	NEW TITLES	TOTAL PROCESSED
TITLE	521 (79.54%)	134 (20.46%)	655 (100.00%)

	ADDED COPIES		NEW TITLES		TOTAL PROCESSED
	VIA SWYL	VIA OCLC	VIA OCLC	ORIG. CAT.	
TITLES	367	154	129	5	655
	(56.03%)	----- (43.21%) -----		(0.76%)	(100.00%)

ber of titles in the monograph collection was later found to be close to 8,000, which is 1,000 more than the original 7,000 represented in the shelf list. Another unforeseen factor which affected the final processing was the presence of titles represented as monographs in the shelf list, which had been cataloged by the main Library as serials–approximately 3% of the monograph collection. The project decision regarding cataloging discrepancies was to accept the main Library's current cataloging practice for each title from the shelf list. Since the cataloging guidelines for this project were established after the shelf list sample was taken, it was impossible to anticipate this occurrence.

PERSONNEL AND COSTS

The fact that this project was a joint venture between the Library and the Computer Science Department enhanced the cooperative spirit on the part of both parties. An average of 8,000-10,000 titles are processed by Automated Services staff each month. Due to the comparatively small number of titles in the Computer Science collection, and the nature of the cataloging involved in this project, the option of integrating most of this project into Automated Services' routine workflow was viewed as most expedient. While the planning team recognized the reality of staff costs to complete the project, the Library was committed to this approach because it involved little or no re-training or re-allocation of staff on a temporary basis. This work was absorbed internally, and represented the Library's contribution to the venture. Fortunately the project was planned to take place during the summer, a non-peak cataloging and processing time. As such, cost estimates for most staff labor were not pertinent.

The Computer Science Department generously offered to share a portion of the processing costs with the Library. The project team decided to calculate both OCLC processing costs and the cost of employing students to perform duties such as initial searching of the Computer Science shelf list, retrieval of shelf list drawers and photocopying title pages in the event that cataloging required more information on a particular title. Cost figures were based on the

TABLE 2. Monograph Shelf List Actual Figures

	ADDED COPIES	NEW TITLES	TOTAL PROCESSED
TITLES	5698 (72.44%)	2168 (27.56%)	7866 (100.00%)
ITEMS	7444	2542	9986

	ADDED COPIES		NEW TITLES		TOTAL PROCESSED
	VIA SWYL	VIA OCLC	VIA OCLC	ORIG. CAT.	
TITLES	3865	1833	1970	198	7866
	(48.13	------- (48.35%) -------		(2.52%)	(100.00%)

type and the amount of processing which was predicted by the shelf list sample.

The project team believed that the PC workstation and software program would simplify searching of the local system and adding of copies to the point where these operations could be performed by a student assistant. The student assistant using the PC workstation had the potential of performing over 50% of the work required to process the collection, since almost 50% of the monographs were added copies, and each of the approximately 7,000 titles from the shelf list would first be searched on the local online system. It was estimated that a student could perform approximately 25 title searches per hour in the local online system, using the PC workstation and software program. Similarly, one can add copies to approximately 70 titles per hour using the LCS SUPERWYLBUR editing program. Table 3 lists the estimated number of hours required for shelf list searching and adding copies to the local system by a student assistant. The Engineering Library also agreed to perform original cataloging and act as the training liaison for the Computer Science Library. Some student hours would be needed to help support the activities in which staff in that library would otherwise be involved. The Computer Science Department agreed to contribute both student wages and an IBM PC with a 20 megabyte hard drive (to be used as the staff PC workstation) to support the project.

The project team also estimated the OCLC costs associated with this endeavor. Table 4, "OCLC Cost Estimates," describes the type of activity, the number of titles involved, the cost per title, and the total estimated cost. These cost figures were based on the 1987-88 non-prime update charge ($1.17) and original cataloging credit (+.50 per record).

THE STAFF PC WORKSTATION

One of the main goals of this project was to create a PC program which could promote local shelf list searching for copy first, using students to quickly process as many added copies as possible, thereby saving time and money. If the title could not be found on the local online system, the second goal of the program was to organize the remaining titles in lists according to the specific unit in Automated Services which needed to further process the titles. With these ideas in mind, Winnie Chan, Automated Services Maintenance Librarian and a member of the project team, developed the program, which was named "CSADD."

The CSADD program was designed to capture the results of the online catalog shelf list searching. CSADD, written in the BASIC interpreter programming language, smoothly performed several

TABLE 3. Student Activities Cost Estimate

ACTIVITY	# HOURS	PAY RATE/HR	COST
LCS/FBR Searching	280 (25 titles/hr., 7000 titles)	$3.25	$910.00
Added Copy	60 (70 titles/hr., 4000 titles)	$3.25	$195.00
Miscellaneous	30 (photocopy, piece retrieval, shelf list retrieval)	$3.25	$97.50
TOTAL	370 hours		$1202.50

TABLE 4. OCLC Cost Estimates*

OCLC Processing	# Titles	Unit Cost	Total Cost
Monographs:			
Updates (non-prime)	3075	$1.17	$3627.00
Original	70	+ .50	+ 35.00
Proceedings:			
Updates (non-prime)	245	$1.17	$286.65
Original	179	+ .50	+ 89.50
Serials:			
Updates (non-prime)	268	$1.17	$313.56
Original	20	+ .50	+ 10.00
TOTAL COST:			**$4092.71**

*Searching costs were assumed to have been negligible due to prevailing search-to-produce ratios at the time (1987).

operations. First, it provided terminal emulation for searching ILLI-NET Online. Second, it downloaded bibliographic and circulation records directly from ILLINET Online (i.e., call number, OCLC number, LCCN), and it prompted the searcher to input various types of information, such as the copy number (assigned by the searcher), or brief bibliographic information from the shelf list card. A third and most important component of CSADD was its capability to produce six output files, depending on the status of the information gleaned from each shelflist card:

1. *Updates:*(true added copies) information sent through the SUPERWYLBUR program to update LCS holdings.
2. *CSLCS*: (half added copies) records which are already in LCS, but required updating on OCLC so they would appear in FBR. The data stored in this file consisted of LCS call number, author, title, publication date, LC card number, and added copy and volume information. Since the LCS call number was provided, the item could easily be updated in OCLC,

if it was found in OCLC. Many of the records in this file were processed without delay.

3. *CSFBR*: (in FBR, not in LCS) data stored in this file included FBR Record Identifier number and the copy/volume information for each volume. The FBR Record Identifier, actually the OCLC number, was easily used to locate the OCLC record, which was passed on to the Copy Cataloging unit for classification.

4. *CSNONE*: (not in FBR or LCS) in this file brief bibliographic information was keyed from the Computer Science shelf list card. This list was used by OCLC searchers, who retrieved many of the titles, and passed them on either to Copy Cataloging for classification, or to Original Cataloging.

5. *CSSERIAL*: Records cataloged as serials by the main Library. Since the holdings information on the shelf list cards was not always complete, these records were saved for later verification.

6. *CSLIST*: A brief record listing of all items searched, generated in Computer Science shelf list order.

The program combined elements of interactive programming to prompt for new data (e.g., holdings) inputting, while it allowed for self-piloted searching of ILLINET Online to retrieve added copy bibliographic and holdings/location records. Three function keys (F1, F5, and F9) were defined for use in capturing and recording information when searching the Computer Science library shelf list against the ILLINET Online database. The program was designed for use by trained undergraduate student assistants. In order to track time spent on a cumulative basis, and to maintain records of work completed by several students who were employed on the project, the program recorded login time, name of terminal operator, and stored the work of each operator in a separate file each day. Those files were then appended at the end of the day, after cursory (human) review for any system or inputting inconsistencies. Each file was named with up to four digits to represent the month and date of inputting (the year was not necessary since the project was completed within one calendar year). Table 5, "Computer Science Recon Project Statistics (Monograph Collection)," details the statis-

TABLE 5. Computer Science RECON Project Statistics (Monograph Collection)

File/Date	Total	In Both	In LCS	In FBR	In Neither	As Serial
625	35	19	5	2	9	0
630	108	54	29	5	19	1
701	84	54	17	0	12	1
702	66	26	14	6	14	6
705	176	60	35	10	57	14
706	137	44	35	2	54	2
707	203	81	37	10	73	2
708	152	73	49	2	20	8
709	198	147	18	1	22	10
710	157	35	85	2	28	7
713	202	69	91	4	31	7
715	205	65	15	7	70	48
716	128	44	62	3	18	1
717	191	63	88	1	33	6
720	30	11	9	2	8	0
721	261	92	105	8	55	1
722	236	105	56	7	67	1
723	276	117	87	4	64	4
724	115	61	27	1	24	2
727	150	81	40	0	28	1
728	144	70	46	5	20	3
729	297	170	43	3	81	0
730	250	104	45	10	88	3
731	151	50	39	8	50	4
802	24	5	5	1	13	0
803	276	89	57	13	107	10
804	279	101	50	17	108	3
805	267	90	45	12	111	9
806	126	66	11	5	40	4
807	291	227	16	2	37	9
810	110	81	12	2	9	6
811	123	101	5	1	11	5

TABLE 5 (continued)

(file/date)	(total)	(in both)	(in LCS)	(in FBR)	(in neither)	(as serial)
812	204	136	29	5	25	9
813	212	150	29	2	25	6
814	103	86	6	0	8	3
817	130	70	34	3	19	4
818	178	138	19	2	17	2
819	117	80	16	7	13	1
820	152	88	32	2	25	5
821	31	11	16	0	2	2
826	155	75	54	0	20	6
827	156	69	48	4	35	0
828	89	41	26	0	21	1
831	161	59	25	2	74	1
901	166	79	4	10	72	1
902	158	64	52	1	39	2
903	170	68	55	1	45	1
904	83	42	20	2	19	0
908	160	56	40	4	56	4
909	88	38	11	4	34	1
910	134	57	42	3	30	2

Titles	8095 **	3862	1836	208	1960	229
Items	9986	4806	2638	------- 2542 -------		N/A
	(100%)	(47.71%)	(22.68%)	(2.57%)	(24.21%)	(2.83%)

** Includes 229 titles which were cataloged as serials:

$$
\begin{array}{r}
8095 \\
- 7866 \\
\hline
229
\end{array}
$$

tical report produced by the program, which maintained a running total, by date (file) of all records input from the Computer Science monograph collection. Column 3, "In both," represents shelf list records which, when searched in ILLINET Online, were found to have a bibliographic (FBR) and a circulation/holdings/location

(LCS) record–added copies which could be updated using the local system's batch mode editor, SUPERWYLBUR. The CSADD program downloaded the bibliographic information from the existing LCS record as the terminal operator searched, and also captured the new volume/copy information and formatted it for processing by the weekly system maintenance batch programs. This file was called "Updates." Columns four and five represent records which were found to be either in LCS or in FBR–added copies which needed updating through OCLC in order for the Library to add its holdings symbol to OCLC, and to automatically produce either an FBR or an LCS record locally. Information from these two columns was actually stored in one of two files, CSFBR or CSLCS, depending on which record was present in the local database. In column six, "In neither" suggests that the record was not found in ILLINET Online; these records were automatically stored in the CSNONE file, printed out, and sent on for OCLC searching, and would either require copy or original cataloging. Column 7, "As serial," refers to the records which were cataloged by the Computer Science Library as monographs, but were cataloged by the Main library as serials. Information from these items was recorded for future processing and placed in the CSSERIAL file.

CSLIST, another output file of the CSADD program, stored the old Computer Science shelf list numbers and the newly-assigned Dewey numbers with holdings and location information. This list was sorted both in CS call number order and Dewey call number order. The two lists were printed, and sent to the Computer Science library once the major portion of the conversion was done so they would have a checklist for their re-marking and collection shifting project.

A student assistant was trained to search the local ILLINET Online catalog using information available on the shelf list card for each item. The program operated in a basic fashion, providing several options for the type of input the searcher might need:

1. Press < ESC > to enter the session;
2. Enter the date of input (e.g., 5/19);
3. Proceed with searching the local catalog (ILLINET Online–LCS & FBR);
4. Press   F1: item in LCS/FBR;
            F5: item in FBR only;

F9: item in LCS only;
F9: item not found;
< ESC > to skip a record or to search it later (e.g., serial);
5. Press "Q" to exit program.

A typical search session might follow this pattern:

1. (a) FBR author search (FIND AUTHOR Quarterman, John#); if results were too large, a Boolean combination with a keyword title search was done (FIND @.A. TITLE matrix);
(b) if author information was not available, or searching was unsuccessful, an FBR keyword title search was done (FIND TITLE matrix);
2. an attempt was made to link the FBR record to the LCS circulation and holdings record;
3. if there was either no FBR record, or no link from an FBR record to its LCS circulation record, an LCS search was done (author/title: ATS/quarmatri; or author: AUT/quartejoh; or title: TLS/matr_____.)

Figure 4, "Shelflist Searching Procedures," describes the decisions and branches the searcher followed to determine whether an existing cataloging record could be found. At the end of the process, the searcher would press one of the three previously defined function keys, depending on what type of information had been retrieved. The three functions fed the input to the six files described earlier. After each function key had been pressed, the searcher would be prompted to supply further information from the shelf list card. In the case of the above example, several prompts enabled the operator to supply bibliographic information from the shelf list card which would be stored in one of the six files and later used for further processing. The three routines operated in the following manner:

F1 Routine (in both LCS and FBR):

1.   Searcher finds FBR and LCS record for shelf list item and presses F1;
2.   Enter CS shelf list number:
(program checks LCS record for serial indicator; if the item is cataloged as a serial in the database, the record is stored in the CSSERIAL file, and later printed out in the CSLIST with this header:

FIGURE 4. Shelflist Searching Procedures

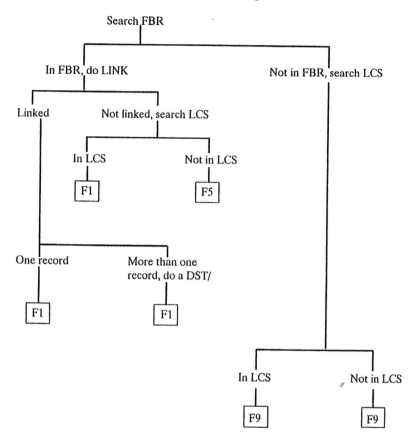

SERIAL RECORD–SAVE FOR LATER (in both)

If the item is not a serial the searcher is prompted to supply copy and volume information to complete the call number and holdings information which is later processed in SUPERWYLBUR;

3. Enter copy number:
4. Enter vol. no.:

Program status line:

DATE: 519   F1 = in LCS/FBR   F5 = FBR only   F9 = others   Total:

F5 Routine (FBR only):

1. Searcher finds a matching record in local system, and presses F5;
2. Enter CS shelf list number:
3. Enter FBR RID:
4. Enter copy no:
5. Enter vol. no.

Program status line:

DATE: 519   F1 = in LCS/FBR   F5 = FBR only   F9 = others   Total:

F9 Routine (in neither):

1. Searcher fails to find a matching record in local system, and presses F9;
2. Enter old shelf list number:
3. In LCS? (Y/N)
4. Enter LC card no. (from shelflist):
5. Enter date of pub. (from shelflist):
6. Enter place:
7. Enter copy no.:
8. Enter vol. no. (or nos.):
9. Enter vol. no. (or nos.):

Program status line:

DATE: 519   F1 = in LCS/FBR   F5 = FBR only   F9 = others   Total:

Each type of information was combined weekly into an updated shelf list for the Computer Science Library, cross-referenced with their old numbers, and information added about the processing status of an item. For example, a partial listing of the CSLIST for July 17:

CSLIST 7/17:
CS No.: Header:
X3.24V261   IN PROCESS———SEARCH LATER   (in neither)
Dewey No.:   LCS CALL NO.: 621.381V281
    SHORT TITLE: INTRODUCTORY
    ELECTRONICS/VAN DER ZIEL, ALDERT/PRENTICE
    HALL/PRENTICE–HALL ELECTRICAL
    ENGINEERING SERIES
    LC=73–3379 1974
Copy & location: C. 1 DCX

X3.34V638   IN PROCESS————READY TO MARK   (in LCS Only)
LCS CALL NO.: 537V28S1968
VAN DER ZIEL, ALDERT 1910–
SOLID STATE PHYSICAL ELECTRONICSEDENG CLIFFS
LC=NOLC   1948
C.2 DCX

X3.24V286N—NL   LCS CALL NO.: 621.38V28N   (in both)
VAN DER ZIEL, ALDERT, 1910–
NOISE: SOURCES, CHARACTERIZATION,
MEASUREMENT.$ENG CLIFFS
LC=71–112911   1970
C.2 DCX

X3.24V374I   IN PROCESS————SEARCH LATER   (in neither)
LCS CALL NO.:621.31921V239I
SHORT TITLE: INTRODUCTION TO MODERN NET-
WORK SYNTHESIS/VAN
VALKENBURG, MAC ELWYN/WILEY
LC=60–10328   1960
C.4 DCX
C.5 DCX

X3.24V374I   IN PROCESS————READY TO MARK   (in LCS only)
LCS CALL NO.: 621.3192V37N
VAN VALKENBURG, MAC ELWYN 1921 –
NETWORK ANALYSIS$ENG CLIFFS
LC=NOLC   1955
C.5 DCX

X3.24V356C   SERIAL RECORD————SAVE FOR LATER   (in both)
LCS CALL NO.: 621.3N75
MONOGRAPHS IN MODERN ELECTRICAL TECHNOLO-
GY$CAMB MA
LC=NOLC   1972
C.3 DCX

CONCLUSION AND OUTCOMES

The complexities of retrospective conversion and re-cataloging necessitate continual tracking and ongoing reconciliation of discrepancies. Using an approach which integrated the project into existing routines helped minimize the need for new and temporary routines. Shelf list sampling was indeed a valuable method which greatly assisted in planning the nature of the project. However, the reader should bear in mind that it is a time-consuming and not always accurate endeavor. Therefore, shelf list sampling might be used as a general guideline rather than as a basis for precise decision-making.

The CSADD program made it possible to save both money and time. The PC workstation and the files produced using the CSADD program provided current and useful information about the status of items in process both for the Library and for the Computer Science Department. First, the built-in series of prompts within CSADD made it possible for a student to make complex comparisons between the Computer Science shelf list cards and the ILLINET Online database. Much of the preliminary shelf list processing, which would normally be performed by staff within a higher class of library technical expertise, could be shifted to this level for this type of recon project. Second, once the student located a record for a shelf list item in the Library's online catalog, the new holdings information from the shelf list card could be easily entered into LCS without the delay of further handling by additional staff. Further, CSADD's centralized list-producing capability saved time, cost for shipping books, and paper in the steps between searching the local online system and searching the OCLC database.

Within the past decade, the PC has progressed from a typewriter's help-mate to a powerful, sophisticated, and customizable front-end for manipulating the output of mainframe library applications. PC software which enables librarians to perform diverse technical functions integrating communications, variable record length, and relational file functions is also readily available and easy to use. Further, the not-too-distant future possibility of importing records directly from OCLC into our local system, and using one PC workstation to search both OCLC and ILLINET Online point to the desirability of continued software development in this area.

BIBLIOGRAPHY

Bookstein, Abraham. "Sampling from Card Files." *Library Quarterly 53:3* (1983): 307-312.

Clark, Sharon E. and Winnie Chan. "Maintenance of an Online Catalog." *Information Technology and Libraries 4:4* (December, 1985): 324-338. .

Fussler, Herman H. and Julien Simon. *Patterns in the Use of Books in Large Research Libraries.* Chicago: University of Chicago Press, 1969.

Henigman, Barbara. "Networking and Authority Control: Online Catalog Authority Control in Illinois." *Information Technology and Libraries 10:1* (March, 1991): 47-54.

Salika, Catherine. "Linking LCS and FBR: Technical Perspective." *Information Technology and Libraries 4:4* (December, 1985): 315-318.

CONTROL ISSUES

Editing Recon Records:
When Is Enough, Enough?
A Selective Review of the Literature

Edward Adrian Lentz

SUMMARY. Many libraries are still conducting, or are contemplating, retrospective conversion (recon) projects in order to automate their catalogues. Unfortunately, many of the records retrieved from bibliographic utilities require some degree of editing in order that they (a) correctly represent items in the local catalogue and (b) conform to local cataloguing standards. There is little disagreement with this argument. But, the extent of editing necessary is highly debatable. The recon literature is reviewed on the issues of quality control, special material formats and collections, and costs.

INTRODUCTION

Retrospective conversion (recon) of library holdings from manually constructed book and card formats to machine-readable data formats has been going on now for at least two decades. For equally long a period librarians have debated how recon projects and the

Edward Adrian Lentz is Technical Librarian, Corporate Library, Insurance Corporation of British Columbia. Mr. Lentz has been involved in a number of recon projects and system migrations.

Correspondence may be addressed to the author care of ICBC Corporate Library, #249-151 West Esplanade, North Vancouver, B.C., Canada V7M 3H9.

resulting products, the records themselves, should be managed. Central to that debate has been the question of how much editing a derived record should be subjected to. Lighthall (1987) identifies "the old issue of whether or not to accept 'as is' someone else's cataloguing or to edit it to suit one's own needs." What underlies Lighthall's subsequent statement, that "it is almost more important to be consistent than to be right,"[1] is a recognition of the need for reasonably stringent standards in dealing with records entering a database.

The need for applying certain standards for the acceptability of data in derived records has never been seriously challenged. But a consensus does not exist on such issues as: how much uniformity should a standard impose; what special requirements should be expected for materials such as serials; and, what cataloguing code should prevail when dealing with pre-AACR2 records. This paper surveys the literature to illustrate the approaches being advocated by theorists and practitioners. As well, the paper surveys the literature for discussions of recon costs, since the labour, machine, and support tool overhead involved in maintaining a standard will undoubtedly affect a library's adherence to such standards.

The need for maintaining standards is as pressing in the realm of recon projects as it is in current cataloguing operations. Recon is not current cataloguing, Hart (1988) states, "nevertheless, solutions for particular problems must be compatible with existing rules and policies."[2] Rules and standards are at their most effective when applied to problem resolution: under normal conditions, whether current cataloguing or recon operations, well formulated rules should be unobtrusive–organic. Juneja (1987) warns that the "card catalog was never a perfect catalog" since no set of cataloguing standards has ever presumed that its ascendancy requires revision of all previous records. Cataloguing standards have been devised to cope with contemporaneous technologies; they are forward, not backward, looking. Juneja's logic is that we should be as tolerant of the machine catalogue as we are of the card catalogue.[3]

But the computer requires adjustment and conformity to a set of protocols. Avram (1975) reminds us that variations of format and data placement in a printed record are tolerable, but such is not the case in "efficient machine processing."[4] Heitshu and Quinn (1985) remark that "standards are necessary in any conversion effort (but) the system used will dictate at least some of these standards or conventions."[5] Computerization, while allowing bibliographical networking, has created an environment in which where data are entered and in what format is as important as what data appear in the record. This means that in designing both databases and standards the librarian must consider how "old" data, recon records, are to be handled in the system. Boss and Espo (1987) point out: "the creation of the database in terms of standards, design, and approaches to retrospective conversion is vital to the long-term success of any library automation project." There are rewards for diligence in accommodating and anticipating file structure requirements: "if properly designed and managed [a] database should outlive several generations of hardware, software, and individual vendors."[6]

Retrospective conversion projects have three levels of usefulness: national, as a source of shared cataloguing on bibliographic utilities; national/regional, to facilitate resource sharing; and, local, in generating products for users.[7] All of these uses–even local–require consistent application of a widely accepted set of standards and guidelines. "Records input into a national database must be as complete and as up to date as possible for future use."[8] This can as easily apply to recon records as to current cataloguing. Even if a library is not inclined to resource sharing, maintenance of the database to an acceptable standard is necessary to facilitate external loading of records.[9] The nature and stringency of the standards chosen to apply to any recon project "will depend on the purpose of the conversion project."[10]

QUALITY CONTROL

Generally, librarians are aware of the need to maintain the integrity of both their own databases and those from which they derive and to which they contribute records.[11,12] Boss and Espo argue that the success of bibliographic utilities arises from that recognition and the utilities' requirements that contributing libraries adhere to standards governing the transcription of data and how the data are encoded.[13] Differences arise though over questions such as: When contributing a recon record to a utility's database, how extensive should the record be?; Should authority work be done on the derived record or are cross-referencing structures in existing authority files adequate for the purpose of conversion?; and, How should bibliographic information which may or may not appear in the derived record be handled?

Crismond (1981) found, after surveying a large number of OCLC users, that those libraries which tended to support the introduction of a cataloguing standard for contributed original records lower than the standard already set for minimal cataloguing in OCLC were libraries with smaller collections and higher percentages of original input. As well, the supporters of lower standards reported that the priority use for their recon records was interlibrary loan, with public access to an on-line catalogue second; the priority was reversed for those supporting higher standards.[14]

How much editing, or quality control, a record is subjected to will often depend on the amount of confidence the library has in whether the shelflist record and the machine record are direct matches and, subsequently, how far the library wants to go in reconciling records. "A 'hit,'" for Gartshore (1987), is "any record recovered which (is) an exact match or one requiring only minor changes such as city of publication (or) edition statement."[15] Hart comments that "usually there is a discrepancy between what the shelflist card says and what the on-line record says."[16] Under these (minor) conditions the library would be inclined to accept a record. Duplicate records in a source database like OCLC can cause problems in verifying a publication since not all LCCNs and ISBNs are unique or accurate.[17] Libraries often search on these two keys only, especially when having their record conversion done commercially.

The literature shows a clear consensus as to how much information a recon record should carry. Kruger (1985) believes that "more is better,"[18] while Bratcher (1987) is convinced that "it is safer to add information from the shelflist card to the on-line record than to delete information from the on-line record to match the shelflist."[19]

This attitude arises not only out of the realization that information deleted is information lost, but as well from a desire on the part of project managers to instill in recon staff a respect for, and trust in, the past work of colleagues.[20,21,22,23] A dissenting opinion regarding the inclination to pool all information residing in the local and utility-based record comes from Juneja who feels that "sometimes a full record taken from a utility can be too full and editing is necessary."[24]

There is general agreement as to which fields in a recon record are most likely to vary from the shelflist record. As well, the literature contains much discussion as to which areas and fields of a record deserve the editor's attention and why. Juneja thinks "fields that can be indexed" are the ones to receive exclusive attention. "Accuracy in these fields is of the utmost importance. Although accuracy in other fields is a nicety, the cost of precision may be greater than the library is willing to consider for the conversion."[25] Kruger agrees in principle by stating that "accurate coding and spelling of the title are crucial to future retrieval of the information."[26] In their review of a serials recon project Heitshu and Quinn found dates of publication and forms of title to cause the most discrepancy and to demand the most editing attention.[27] Hart provides a useful list of common conflicts between machine and shelflist records: dates, editions, reprints, typographical errors, local binding together of separately published items—all of which require editing.[28] Johnson (1982) identifies conflicts in records in terms of categories. Conflicts in access points, name forms, and publishing dates are major concerns; (slight) conflicts regarding pagination and printing dates are minor concerns.[29]

In the same vein as Juneja, Johnson identifies those MARC tags (010, 090/092, 1XX, 245, 250, 260, 300, 4XX, 5XX, 6XX, 7XX, 8XX) which must be checked when verifying a match and reconciled as soon as possible.[30] It must be pointed out here that although Johnson includes the LCCN tag (010), the ISBN tag (020) is ignored. This is curious since the ISBN is more likely to be unique to a single edition of a work. Coincidentally, part of Crismond's survey results indicate that librarians who are inclined to support lower standards for original input of recon records in OCLC favour making LCCNs and ISBNs, as well as all statements of responsibility and uniform titles, non-obligatory.[31] What these librarians refuse to acknowledge, and Crismond does not state, is that without these four points of machine verification in particular, the record is virtually lost to any future recon effort by subscribing libraries.

Boss and Espo warn that "libraries wishing to maximize the benefits of accessing shared bibliographic files must adhere" to standards embodied in AACR2[32] (and, of course, further refined in AACR2R). Not many libraries are heeding the warning in conducting their recon projects. Although, as Reid and Wells (1987) point out, "retrospective conversion offers technical services librarians a golden opportunity to standardize and upgrade records–at a time when few libraries can afford to do so"[33]–most project managers view the idea of bringing old records into line with new ones as pedantic. The literature is awash with statements of compromise and policies of expediency. It does not help matters when, as Kruger and Heitshu and Quinn report, RLIN does not require any kind of adherence to AACR2 or ISBD formatting in recon records as long as the records are coded as substandard.[34,35] Because of this lack of policy, a decision has been made not to update or correct "pre-AACR2 access points."[36] Heitshu and Quinn report that "no attempt was made to change forms of entry to AACR2" in their project.[37] In the project which Copeland (1988) reports on, "all the records that were to be converted were pre-AACR2 records and ISBD punctuation had not been used." Therefore, since the intention was to replicate the card catalogue in machine form, AACR2/ISBD records were derived only if records in a contemporary format did not exist. The rationale for the decision was that updating would require costly alteration to pre-existing print files.[38] Amid a prevailing attitude that the standard which was in place when the record was originally created should be the one adhered to, Banach and Spell (1988) and Hart report a contrary policy at the University of Massachusetts which requires the current cataloguing rules to be applied to recon records.[39,40]

The attitude of expediency tends to be popular regarding authorities for, and the formatting of, traditional access points: main and added entries, and subject headings. In 1975 Avram said that any future amalgamation of the multiple data bases [of the Library of Congress subscribing libraries) into a single unified national data base would entail a formidable task of human editing to make the name and subject headings assigned by many libraries consistent with authorized forms.[41]

Expediency, the desire to let someone else do it, and tight budgets have conspired to make Avram's ideal impractical. But the compromises which are in place are well-intentioned. Systems have been put in place in most cases which recognize the primacy of the local authority file.[42,43,44,45] Where they are available, machine systems which effect global authority changes are being relied upon.[46,47] Where extra subject headings or added entries appear on matching records, headings are being pooled rather than any standard being applied regarding the appropriateness of any given heading.[48,49,50,51] Projects often just do not have the staff or budget to perform more than spot checks on such things as whether subject headings are obsolete. Finally, the machine environment has, over the last few years, caused the "main entry" to become a less than distinct bibliographic entity in the minds of many. It is this "level playing field" attitude toward access points which, I suspect, motivates in part such policies as the one Kruger reports which accepts as the "main" entry whatever entry qualified according to the "cataloging rules that were applied by the RLIN member library."[52]

One important aspect of the issue of editing recon records that has received scant attention in the literature is the reconciliation of variant classification numbers assigned to local and source records. This is disturbing since it is more likely that libraries will have assigned variant class numbers to items on the basis of local subject emphases than it is that irreconcilable subject headings will have been assigned. It is easily conceivable that libraries can end up with large portions of particular subject collections far removed physically because of adherence to policies requiring unquestioned acceptance of call numbers in source records. As well, as Arcand (1986) points out, classification numbers are subject to redefinition.[53] This can lead to shelving incongruities. In the absence of appropriate policies on the issue, libraries can easily find themselves confronted with embarrassing inquiries from their clientele. As Lighthall (1988) puts it: "The advantages of a 'clean' consistent shelf arrangement and of reconciling the difficulties of having materials on the same general topic in different places on the shelves are obvious."[54]

SPECIAL MATERIALS

Conflicts between machine records and the local records they are matched with in a conversion project often arise through variations in the handling of special materials such as loose-leaf publications,[55] rare books, music scores, and serials. Non-monographic materials invariably require more stringent standards and procedures for both verification and editing of recon records.

Johnson reports on the experience of performing retrospective conversion on a rare book collection. Few discrepancies between local and source records were encountered because of the consistently high standards applied to the cataloguing of these materials over the years. Subsequently, of the three databases constructed during the recon project, the rare book database was the most complete and had relatively "fewer errors." This collection also netted a lower per unit cost "because of the high quality of cataloging and the use of experienced staff."[56]

The conversion of music scores probably presents the greatest opportunity for frustration and error in any project. "Verifying uniform titles" is the most important logistical concern with this material type. Because of the limited search capabilities of bibliographic utilities "more time (is spent) in the conversion process" verifying matches and subsequently editing hits to account for subtle distinctions in varying manifestations of a score. Bratcher reports a high hit rate on a very small collection. The standards applied in the project reported on were generally higher than the norm reported in this paper.

> All fields were compared and edited to match the shelflist card or the score itself. In addition, name/title/subject access points were verified and converted to AACR2 form if necessary. A professional cataloger was used to convert all records. . . . [57]

The conversion of serial records is the most widely reviewed process in the literature *vis-à-vis* the treatment of special materials. This can be attributed to the fact that "probably the most significant way in which a record gets changed is when recataloging is required of its title entry."[58] Heitshu and Quinn expand on this point to give an impression of the logistical nightmare that awaits the manager of a serials recon, as well as reviewing the options available when attempting to reconcile local and derived records:

> Because serial publications are not static, but change titles, merge, split, and supersede one another, decisions must be made about how to adequately represent these variations bibliographically. The most significant of these decisions is the use of successive-versus-latest title cataloging. . . .
>
> The first option, which might be described as the ideal, would involve recataloging a great many titles and would require extensive piece checks and original cataloging when a record was not available on-line in order to create reliable successive records. . . .
>
> Option two would involve converting the catalog record exactly as it existed. This option would require a minimum amount of recataloging. . . .

Option three would assign a cut-off date at which all titles catalogued prior to it would be edited according to latest entry principles, while all titles catalogued after the cut off would be edited for successive entry. "This compromise reflect(s) a recognition of the importance of successive cataloging, as well as a realization that total recataloging with successive records [is] an impossibility."[59] In contrast to the cut-off date approach, Copeland (1988) reports that the decision to catalogue successively or by latest-entry methods depended predominantly on the shelf list and, secondarily, on whether a matching machine record was available:

> If the shelflist indicated that a serial had been cataloged under latest entry conventions, one option was to use latest entry cataloging records from the database and/or input original latest entry cataloging. . . .

> If the title on the shelflist card was 'latest entry' cataloging and the only records in the database were successive entries, the catalogers chose, in most cases, to input a new record based on the shelflist card.[60]

The overwhelming importance of this issue to the whole recon process is clear when viewed in the light of the warning by Spalding (1954) that "it takes 50 percent longer to recatalog than to catalog originally."[61]

COSTS

Port (1973) states that "editing has been one of the costlier aspects of the data preparation process."[62] This early opinion has been borne out over the years in the literature. Peters and Butler report a cost model developed to compare alternative conversion methods. Their results show that, whether the conversion is conducted in-house or contracted out to a vendor, for a 100,000 title project the cost of verifying matches and subsequently editing records accounts for over half of the total cost of the project.[63]

The labour costs which accrue to the editing component of any project will depend largely "upon the level of compensation of the staff assigned the task."[64] Johnson feels it is "more cost-efficient to have paraprofessionals rather than student assistants edit and update database records."[65]

In costing a project, considerations going far beyond labour and equipment must be made. Many of these considerations involve the impact of standards set for the project and the extensiveness of editing arising from these standards. Boss and Espo point out that "conversion of nonstandard files . . . require[s] special conversion programs that must be charged to a single library."[66] Port observes that "one factor that distorts cost data is the question of quality control. The type and number of errors are often not specifically identified and additional correction costs" may not be articulated.[67] Even though editing costs may be buried and hard to root out into the open, efforts have been made to characterize those costs. Peters and Butler identify four "distinct categories of records." They are:

1. Acceptable as is. 2. Minor editing needed (changing existing call numbers and headings, correcting misspellings). 3. Major editing required (adding fields of all types or fixed field coding). 4. Not matched in database.[68]

Each category of record exacts a different cost in terms of processing time and staff effort.

CONCLUSION

In 1969 one of the conclusions of the Library of Congress's RECON Working Task Force was that

> conversion for a national bibliographic data base requires standardization of bibliographic content and machine format. Standards for conversion of retrospective records should be the same as those for current records.[69]

By 1973 there was an

> unresolved question . . . concerning the level of complexity of bibliographic description and format that provides optimum use of a machine-readable record. Obviously the Library of Congress is committed to a higher level of detail in maintaining a national/international standard than might be the case for a smaller general library.[70]

What was essentially a speculation on Port's part has flourished to become a fact of life. The whole process of retrospective conversion has been unlucky historically, in the sense that just as libraries came to realize the necessity of taking advantage of, by now, established technologies the money started to dry up. Librarians maintain that they would like to adhere to lofty international standards but compromises must be made to stay within budgets. But a Catch-22 is apparent in that many major, large-scale, conversions are "funded with the understanding that certain national standards will be followed."[71]

Librarians must become aware that the only position of integrity available to them is the one paraphrased in the saying: "I can do it now . . . or I can do it right." It is only honest to concede that "the most important and most often unstated assumption [of recon] is the library's attitude on the quality *versus* quantity issue." Hart goes on to comment that "if the library has opted for a 'quick and dirty' project" there is likely to be little editing of records done. "On the other hand, if a library is using retrospective conversion as a chance to clean up its catalog, the problem resolution phase will resemble a recataloging project."[72] Both of these circumstances are obviously extreme.

It is hard to conceive of the editing process being compromised without negative consequences. In another context, Lighthall remarks that "effective access to the collection . . . will not be realized if all the old inconsistencies and limitations . . . are perpetuated."[73] The sentiment is apt in the present context. Banach and Spell admit that "quick and dirty conversion . . . would make any subsequent linking project difficult and might take years to clean up."[74]

> The editing procedure is the heart of the conversion process; quality in a recon project is attained only through consistent editing decisions and the development of rules and standards against which the bibliographic information can be evaluated.[75]

NOTES

1. Lynne Lighthall, "Strategies for Automating the Card Catalogue: The Vancouver Experience," *School Libraries in Canada* 7 (Winter 1987): 31.

2. Amy Hart, "Operation Cleanup: The Problem Resolution Phase of a Retrospective Conversion," *Library Resources & Technical Services* 32 (Oct. 1988): 379.

3. Derry C. Juneja, "Quality Control in Data Conversion," *Library Resources & Technical Services* 31 (Apr./June 1987): 158.

4. Allen Kent and others, eds. *Encyclopedia of Library and Information Sciences* vol. 16 (New York: Dekker, 1975), s.v. "Machine-Readable Cataloguing (MARC) Program," by Henriette D. Avram.

5. Sara C. Heitshu and Joan M. Quinn, "Serials Conversion at the University of Michigan," *Drexel Library Quarterly* 21 (Winter 1985): 68.

6. Richard W. Boss and Hal Espo, "Standards, Database Design, & Retrospective Conversion," *Library Journal* 112 (Oct. 1, 1987): 54.

7. Heitshu and Quinn, "Serials Conversion at the University of Michigan," 62.

8. Carolyn A. Johnson, "Retrospective Conversion of Three Library Collections," *Information Technology and Libraries* 1 (June 1982), 133.

9. Boss and Espo, "Standards, Database Design, & Retrospective Conversion," 55.

10. Stephen H. Peters and Douglas J. Butler, "A Cost Model for Retrospective Conversion Alternatives," *Library Resources & Technical Services* 28 (Apr./June 1984): 162.

11. Linda F. Crismond, "Quality Issues in Retrospective Conversion Projects," *Library Resources & Technical Services* 25 (Jan./Mar. 1981): 48-55.

12. Juneja, "Quality Control in Data Conversion," 148.

13. Boss and Espo, "Standards, Database Design, & Retrospective Conversion," 54.

14. Crismond, "Quality Issues in Retrospective Conversion," 50.

15. Tom Gartshore, "BiblioFile and the School Library," *School Libraries in Canada* 7 (Winter 1987): 38.

16. Hart, "Operation Cleanup," 379.

17. Juneja, "Quality Control in Data Conversion," 155.

18. Kathleen Joyce Kruger, "MARC Tags and Retrospective Conversion: The Editing Process," *Information Technology and Libraries* 4 (Mar. 1985): 54.

19. Perry Bratcher, "Music OCLC Recon: The Practical Approach," *Cataloging & Classification Quarterly* 8(2) (1987/88): 46.

20. Johnson, "Retrospective Conversion of Three Library Collections," 133-9.

21. Kruger, "MARC Tags and Retrospective Conversion," 53-7.

22. Heitshu and Quinn, "Serials Conversion at the University of Michigan," 62-76.

23. Nora S. Copeland, "Retrospective Conversion of Serials: The RLIN Experience," *Serials Review* 14(3) (1988): 25.

24. Juneja, "Quality Control in Data Conversion," 152.

25. Ibid., 156.

26. Kruger, "MARC Tags and Retrospective Conversion," 55.

27. Heitshu and Quinn, "Serials Conversion at the University of Michigan," 71.

28. Hart, "Operation Cleanup," 380-3.

29. Johnson, "Retrospective Conversion of Three Library Collections," 136.

30. Ibid., 135.

31. Crismond, "Quality Issues in Retrospective Conversion," 50-1.

32. Boss and Espo, "Standards, Database Design, & Retrospective Conversion," 54.

33. Marion T. Reid and Kathleen L. Wells, "Retrospective Conversion: Through the Looking Glass," *RTSD Newsletter* 12 (Winter 1987): 11.

34. Kruger, "MARC Tags and Retrospective Conversion," 56.

35. Heitshu and Quinn, "Serials Conversion at the University of Michigan," 67-8.

36. Kruger, "MARC Tags and Retrospective Conversion," 56.

37. Heitshu and Quinn, "Serials Conversion at the University of Michigan," 70.

38. Copeland, "Retrospective Conversion of Serials," 24-6.

39. Patricia Banach and Cynthia Spell, "Serials Conversion at the University of Massachusetts at Amherst," *Information Technology and Libraries* 7 (June 1988): 128-9.

40. Hart, "Operation Cleanup," 385.

41. Kent, *Encyclopedia of Library and Information Sciences*, 387 (vol. 16).

42. Michael T. Krieger, "Retrospective Conversion in a Two-Year College," *Information Technology and Libraries* 1 (Mar. 1982): 43.

43. Johnson, "Retrospective Conversion of Three Library Collections," 135-6.

44. Banach and Spell, "Serials Conversion at the University of Massachusetts at Amherst," 127, 129.

45. Bratcher, "Music OCLC Recon," 44.

46. Copeland, "Retrospective Conversion of Serials," 24.

47. Lynne Lighthall, "A Planning and Implementation Guide for Automating School Libraries: Implementing a System (Part II)," *School Libraries in Canada* 8 (Summer 1988): 44-5.

48. Krieger, "Retrospective Conversion in a Two-Year College," 43.

49. Heitshu and Quinn, "Serials Conversion at the University of Michigan," 70.

50. Banach and Spell, "Serials Conversion at the University of Massachusetts at Amherst," 126.

51. Kruger, "MARC Tags and Retrospective Conversion," 56.

52. Ibid., 55-6.

53. Janet Arcand, "A Serials Cataloger's Work is Never Done," *Serials Librarian* 10 (Summer 1986): 38.

54. Lighthall, "A Planning and Implementation Guide for Automating School Libraries," 44.

55. Banach and Spell, "Serials Conversion at the University of Massachusetts at Amherst," 129.

56. Johnson, "Retrospective Conversion of Three Library Collections," 133-9.

57. Bratcher, "Music OCLC Recon," 43, 47.

58. Arcand, "A Serials Cataloger's Work is Never Done," 37.

59. Heitshu and Quinn, "Serials Conversion at the University of Michigan," 68-9.

60. Copeland, "Retrospective Conversion of Serials," 25, 27.

61. C. Sumner Spalding, *Certain Proposals of Numerical Systems for the Control of Serials Evaluated for Their Application at the Library of Congress*, (Washington, D.C.: Library of Congress, Serial Record Division, 1954) cited in Arcand, "A Serials Cataloger's Work is Never Done," 36.

62. Idelle Port, "Developing a Strategy for Retrospective Conversion of the Card Catalog to a Machine-Readable Data Base in Three Academic Libraries (Small, Medium and Large)," *Information Storage and Retrieval* 9 (1973): 270.

63. Peters and Butler, "A Cost Model for Retrospective Conversion Alternatives," 159-60.

64. Ibid., 156.

65. Johnson, "Retrospective Conversion of Three Library Collections," 139.

66. Boss and Espo, "Standards, Database Design, & Retrospective Conversion," 55.

67. Port, "Developing a Strategy for Retrospective Conversion," 272.

68. Peters and Butler, "A Cost Model for Retrospective Conversion Alternatives," 154.

69. Kent, *Encyclopedia of Library and Information Sciences*, 388 (vol. 16).

70. Port, "Developing a Strategy for Retrospective Conversion," 269.

71. Heitshu and Quinn, "Serials Conversion at the University of Michigan," 68.

72. Hart, "Operation Cleanup," 384.

73. Lighthall, "A Planning and Implementation Guide for Automating School Libraries," 44.

74. Banach and Spell, "Serials Conversion at the University of Massachusetts at Amherst," 125.

75. Kruger, "MARC Tags and Retrospective Conversion," 53.

BIBLIOGRAPHY

Arcand, Janet. "A Serials Cataloger's Work is Never Done." *Serials Librarian* 10:35-43 (Summer 1986).

Banach, Patricia, and Cynthia Spell. "Serials Conversion at the University of Massachusetts at Amherst." *Information Technology and Libraries* 7:124-30 (June 1988).

Boss, Richard W., and Espo, Hal. "Standards, Database Design, & Retrospective Conversion." *Library Journal* 112:54-8 (Oct. 1, 1987).

Bratcher, Perry. "Music OCLC Recon: The Practical Approach." *Cataloging & Classification Quarterly* 8(2) 41-8 (1987/88).

Copeland, Nora S. "Retrospective Conversion of Serials: The RLIN Experience." *Serials Review* 14(3):23-8 (1988).

Crismond, Linda F. "Quality Issues in Retrospective Conversion Projects." *Library Resources and Technical Services* 25:48-55 (Jan./Mar. 1981).

Gartshore, Tom. "BiblioFile and the School Library." *School Libraries in Canada* 7:36-40 (Winter 1987).

Hart, Amy. "Operation Cleanup: The Problem Resolution Phase of a Retrospective Conversion Project." *Library Resources & Technical Services* 32:378-86 (Oct. 1988).

Heitshu, Sara C., and Joan M. Quinn. "Serials Conversion at the University of Michigan." *Drexel Library Quarterly* 21:62-76 (Winter 1985).

Johnson, Carolyn A. "Retrospective Conversion of Three Library Collections." *Information Technology and Libraries* 1:133-9 (June 1982).

Juneja, Derry C. "Quality Control in Data Conversion." *Library Resources & Technical Services* 31:148-58 (Apr./June 1987).

Kent, Allen, and others, eds. *Encyclopedia of Library and Information Sciences.* Vol. 16. New York: Dekker, 1975. S.v. "Machine-Readable Cataloging (MARC) Program," by Henriette O. Avram.

Krieger, Michael T. "Retrospective Conversion in a Two-Year College." *Information Technology and Libraries* 1:41-4 (March 1982).

Kruger, Kathleen Joyce. "MARC Tags and Retrospective Conversion: The Editing Process." *Information Technology and Libraries* 4:53-7 (Mar. 1985).

Lighthall, Lynne. "A Planning and Implementation Guide for Automating School Libraries: Implementing a System (Part II)." *School Libraries in Canada* 8:42-7 (Summer 1988).

Lighthall, Lynne. "Strategies for Automating the Card Catalogue: The Vancouver Experience." *School Libraries in Canada* 7:27-33 (Winter 1987).

Peters, Stephen H., and Douglas J. Butler. "A Cost Model for Retrospective Conversion Alternatives." *Library Resources and Technical Services* 28:149-62 (Apr./June 1984).

Port, Idelle. "Developing a Strategy for Retrospective Conversion of the Card Catalog to a Machine-Readable Data Base in Three Academic Libraries (Small, Medium and Large)." *Information Storage and Retrieval* 9:267-80 (1973).

Reed-Scott, Jutta. "Retrospective Conversion: An Update." *American Libraries* 16:694-8 (Nov. 1985).

Reid, Marion T., and Kathleen L. Wells. "Retrospective Conversion: Through the Looking Glass." *RTSD Newsletter* 12:10-11 (Winter 1987).

Spalding, C. Sumner. *Certain Proposals of Numerical Systems for the Control of Serials Evaluated for Their Application at the Library of Congress.* Washington: D.C.: Library of Congress, Serial Record Division, 1954.

Managing Authority Control
in a Retrospective Conversion Project

James Tilio Maccaferri

SUMMARY. Authority control is an essential component of the retrospective conversion process. Libraries contemplating authority control in this context need to consider the source of the converted records, the nature of the collection being converted, when and by whom the source records were cataloged, and the extent to which the converted records should approach local authority control standards. Choices for processing these records include manual and machine techniques or a combination of the two, while the actual work may be done in-house, by a vendor, or by dividing the work between local staff and a vendor. Decisions on which techniques and approaches to use will depend on local resources and standards.

Several decades' experience with library automation has demonstrated that authority control is at least as important in an online catalog as it is in a card or book catalog. In fact, many would say that it is more important in an online environment, given the literalness of computer filing and searching. The renewed interest in authority control which this finding has sparked is apparent both in the growth of literature on authority control and in the development of increasingly sophisticated authority control features in online catalogs. Far less attention has been paid to the problems of applying authority control on the bibliographic records produced through retrospective conversion, even though retrospective conversion is an essential step in each library's migration from a manual to an online catalog. Just as there are many retrospective conversion options

James Tilio Maccaferri, PhD, is Assistant Professor, Department of Library Science, Clarion University of Pennsylvania, Clarion, PA 16214-1232.

145

available to libraries, so it is too with retrospective authority control. Given the many variables involved, it is impossible to be prescriptive with respect to this process. The following discussion is therefore limited to considering the objectives of authority control, the degree to which it is needed in the retrospective conversion process, and the major options available to libraries in implementing authority control in this context. While this discussion assumes that libraries will use the name and subject authority files of the Library of Congress (LC), the management considerations are essentially the same regardless of which authority records are used.

Authority control is about consistency. It seeks to insure that the name, uniform title, and subject headings used on bibliographic records are unique, uniform, and correctly formulated. It accomplishes these tasks by distinguishing terms, identifying relationships between terms, formulating headings and references for these terms in accordance with established rules, and then documenting this work by creating authority records containing the authorized or "established" heading, any references, and supporting information. In addition to these intellectual activities, authority control also involves editing headings on existing bibliographic and authority records to achieve consistency. Authority control advances both the finding and collocating functions of the catalog–the former by providing references from alternate forms of names and by introducing a degree of certainty into searches; the latter by bringing together under one heading all works associated with a given person, body, uniform title, or subject.[1]

Achieving the objectives of authority control is difficult even for current cataloging in a single library. Heading uniformity may suffer due to carelessness on the part of catalogers. Since topical subject headings are drawn from authorized lists, they at least should always be unique; but this is not necessarily the case with name headings. Name headings are based on actual usage, and, when the names of different persons or works are identical, uniqueness can only be achieved by adding a qualifying term. If such terms are unavailable, undifferentiated name headings must be tolerated.[2] Formulating headings correctly means applying the proper rules, such as those found in the second edition of *Anglo-American Cataloguing Rules (AACR2)* or LC's *Subject Cataloging Manual*. Even where this is a requirement for new cataloging, catalog managers may balk at reformulating existing headings to bring them into compliance with current rules. Implementing *AACR2* was especially challenging in this respect, since this code's rules for name and title headings vary greatly in principle and detail from those of earlier ones.[3] *Library of Congress Subject Headings (LCSH)* has not experienced as drastic a transformation, but the ongoing addition, deletion, and replacement of individual subject headings and subdivisions necessitate a good deal of catalog maintenance. As costly as this maintenance may be, failing to update headings can have serious consequences for users, especially with regard to subject headings, since failing to follow current LC practice threatens the integrity of the catalog's syndetic structure.

Retrospective authority control must deal with all of the above considerations and more. The volume of work will be enormous, since the typical retrospective conversion project will involve tens if not hundreds of thousands of headings, all of which must be vetted for uniqueness, uniformity, and, to at least some extent, correctness. Unless the library does not have an authority file, appropriate authority records will also have to be acquired or created and then added to the local online authority file. While many headings will match established headings or references on existing LC or local authority records, a large number will not.[4] Dealing with these unmatched headings is the principal challenge in retrospective authority control.

The number of unmatched headings a library encounters in retrospective authority control will depend in part on the source of the converted records. Manually keying one's own bibliographic records will not guarantee the same degree of authority control present in the manual catalog. Input errors aside, unless a library has consistently updated tracings as well as actual headings, the manually keyed records will probably contain even more discrepancies. Since few libraries update headings on shelflist entries, keying records from this source would result in even more problems. Even for records keyed from a well-maintained catalog, the greater degree of authority control demanded by online systems will probably require some authority processing of the converted records.

In any case, most libraries doing retrospective conversion will obtain their machine readable records from a bibliographic utility. The authority control problems found in a single catalog are magnified in shared bibliographic databases such as those maintained by the utilities, since the records in these databases represent the various and varying cataloging practices of many libraries over many years. Two studies of subject headings in the OCLC database identified four specific categories of errors: (1) inconsistency in spacing, punctuation, and capitalization; (2) typographical and minor spelling errors; (3) invalid forms of headings; and (4) incorrect MARC coding.[5] That these categories are also applicable to name and title headings is shown by the following examples, all of which were found by browsing a database consisting of retrospectively converted records not yet subjected to authority control:[6]

Tawney, R. H. (Richard Henry), 1880-1962. [*AACR2* LC heading]
Tawney, Richard Henry [local variant]
Tawny, Richard Henry, 1880- [local variant]
Tawney, Richard Henry, 1880-1962. [pre-*AACR2* LC heading]

Taylor, A. J. P. (Alan John Percival), 1906- [typographical error]
Taylor, A. J. P. (Alan John Percivale), 1906- [*AACR2* LC heading]
Taylor, Alan John Percivale, 1906- [pre-*AACR2* LC heading]

Comaromi, John P. (John Phillip), 1937- [*AACR2* LC heading]
Comaromi, John Phillip. [local variant]
Comaromi, John Phillip, 1937- [pre-*AACR2* LC heading]

Bible. N.T. Apocryphal books. English. 1963. [AACR2 heading coded as a name]

Bible. English. 1903. Authorized. [pre-*AACR2* heading]
Bible English. Authorized. 1958. [*AACR2* heading]

Turkey–Descr. & trav. [obsolete abbreviation]
Turkey–Description and travel. [*LCSH* heading]

Turkish literature (Collections) [invalid form]
Turkish literature. [*LCSH* heading]

U.S. Atomic Energy Commission. [*AACR2* LC heading]
United States. Atomic Energy Commission. [pre-*AACR2* LC heading]

U. S. Bureau of aeronautics (Navy dept.) [pre-*AACR2* heading with irregular spacing and capitalization]
United States. Navy Dept. Bureau of Aeronautics. [*AACR2* LC heading]

U.S. Bureau of American Ethnology. [pre-*AACR2* heading]
United States. Bureau of American Ethnology. [pre-*AACR2* LC heading]
Smithsonian Institution. Bureau of American Ethnology. [*AACR2* LC heading]

The number of such discrepancies found in any particular database will depend in part on the utility's cataloging standards and on whether the utility's database is itself under authority control.[7]

Other factors affecting the extent to which any particular set of converted records will require authority clean-up are the nature of the library's collection and when and by whom the source records were cataloged. Pre-*AACR2* non-LC records will obviously contain a higher percentage of problem headings than current LC records. Headings on records for special materials, such as law and music, may also contain a disproportionate number of errors due to the problems inherent in cataloging such materials.[8] The same is probably true of foreign language materials. More research, however, is required to confirm these assumptions and thereby provide libraries with better data for planning purposes.

The difficulties encountered in controlling headings on current cataloging and the special problems in dealing with retrospective records raise the question of just how good a library's authority control can or should be. The only way to guarantee unique, uniform, and correct headings is to examine each record–if not each item–individually. This is at least feasible for original cataloging, but copy cataloging efficiency would be impaired if headings on existing bibliographic records were evaluated routinely. For new cataloging, the bibliographic item is at least readily available for inspection. Physical inspection of the item is clearly impractical when dealing with converted records for all but the smallest collections. Consequently, even libraries with high authority control standards for current cataloging may need to adopt more relaxed standards for retrospective records. Before commencing a retrospective conversion project, a library therefore first needs to define its quality standards for authority control and then to determine the degree to which the converted records should approach these standards. Decisions on these points will necessarily inform subsequent choices regarding the means of bringing the retrospective records under authority control.

Decisions must also be made with respect to which authority records a library requires, what information those records should contain, and the means of adding the records to the local authority file. In making these decisions, libraries should be guided by the needs and capabilities of their online system and not just by past practice. Also, instances in which locally created records will be used in lieu of existing LC records need to be identified and the consequences of such decisions accepted. Libraries typically need more authority records than they have unique headings in their bibliographic records due to the hierarchical structure of references. This structure means, for example, that "see" references for the heading "United States" will appear only on the authority record for that heading and not on records for its subordinate and related bodies. This is also the case with subdivided subject headings. The only way to obtain these needed references is to acquire the authority record for the parent body or main subject heading, even if these headings do not appear by themselves on any bibliographic records in the local catalog. Where "see also" references are involved, libraries need to determine whether they wish to include blind references, that is, references to a heading not used on any entries in the local catalog. This is especially a problem for subject authorities, since most libraries use only a subset of *LCSH*. Traditionally, libraries have avoided blind references for both name and subject headings; but there is some sentiment in favor of including at least some blind references for subject headings in the interests of expanding entry vocabulary.[9] A further consideration is whether to include authority records for headings without any references. This was rarely done in manual catalogs due to the effort involved; but adding and maintaining such records online is feasible. The presence of such records confirms that the headings in question are under authority control and may help to distinguish between entities with similar names.

Manual authority records often contained minimal information in an effort to reduce costs; but this may be neither necessary nor desirable in online authority files. With regard to "see" references, libraries should be guided in part by the needs of the local system and the extent to which these needs are met by LC authority records. One factor to consider here is how the local system normalizes headings for searching. Does it, for instance, treat headings such as "U.S." "U. S.," and "US" differently? Other types of references may be redundant, especially in systems with keyword searching.[10] In departing from LC standards, however, one should not underestimate the time required to add or delete references from LC authority records, even for current cataloging. Such an undertaking could prove prohibitive in the context of retrospective conversion. References, of course, are not the only data elements found in authority records. There are also source citations, notes, control codes, and series treatment decisions, among others.[11] Again, past practice was constrained by the cost of maintaining manual files. In an automated system, there is less reason to delete such elements from LC records, and source citations and notes may be essential for identification purposes in assuring that headings are always used appropriately. If a library does decide to dispense with some data elements, consideration should be given to having the local system strip unwanted fields from the record during uploading. Libraries that obtain authority records from a vendor should be aware of any special data, such as local control numbers, that the authority records will require to link properly with the bibliographic records.[12]

When adding authority records to the local online authority file, libraries may choose between manual data entry and machine transfer of records. The former approach will be slow and prone to keying errors.[13] The latter depends on access to LC authority records in machine readable form. If the library has access to an online file of LC authority records, direct system-to-system transfer may be possible.[14] Alternately, it may be possible to download records onto a floppy disk for subsequent uploading into the local system.[15] If a vendor is used for authority processing, the library will probably receive its authority records on magnetic tape. In all cases involving use of machine readable authority records, attention must be paid to the format of the incoming records, since not all systems implement the MARC authorities format identically if at all.[16] Even if the record format is compatible with local system requirements, unforeseen problems may interfere with tape loading routines.[17]

Authority processing of the converted records will involve attempting to match assigned headings with headings in an authority file, verifying those headings which match an authorized heading, changing those which match a "see" reference, identifying for subsequent review those headings which do not match anything, identifying all needed authority records, and ultimately, adding the appropriate authority records to the local authority file--all in accordance with whatever local standards the library establishes. This work may be done manually, by machine, or by a combination of the two. Manual editing cannot compete with machine processing in terms of consistency or speed, whereas machines cannot as yet perform the intellectual aspects of authority control, including discriminating between similar but different headings, editing headings to conform with current cataloging rules, identifying needed references, and doing research to resolve conflicts. If correctness and appropriateness are important criteria in a library's authority control program, a large degree of manual inspection and editing will be required. Machine processing, on the other hand, can deal quickly with a variety of common authority control problems. Uniqueness checks, by which identical character strings are matched, can be used both to validate headings for which authority records already exist and to identify headings which match "see" references. In the latter case, some systems can automatically change the unauthorized heading into its authorized form. Other automated authority control features include hierarchical checks, reciprocity checks, and dependent field validation. Hierarchical checks can determine whether the parent body of a corporate body entered subordinately, the name component of a name/title heading, or the main heading in a subdivided subject heading are represented in the authority file. Reciprocity checks can determine whether a "see also" reference on one authority record matches an established heading (MARC 1XX field) on another authority record. Dependent field validation is the capability to cross-check between MARC fields for the presence of required data.[18]

As desirable as automated authority control features are, it must be emphasized that the algorithms doing this work cannot determine whether matching character strings represent the same entity–it is authority control "With the form conforming duly, / Senseless what it meaneth truly."[19] The blunders such algorithms can produce may be humorous and obvious, such as OCLC's inadvertent transformation of the heading "Madonna" (in this case denoting the entertainer) into "Mary, Blessed Virgin, Saint";[20] but in other cases they will be more subtle.[21] Especially ripe for such errors are corporate names, since, prior to *AACR2*, cataloging rules called for the predominant form or most recent form of the body's name to be used on all records, while *AACR2* requires the cataloger to "establish a new heading under the new name for items appearing under that name."[22] Pre-*AACR2* bibliographic records may thus have corporate headings which match a heading or reference in the LC authority file but which will be inappropriate for the bibliographic record in question. The multiple headings mandated for some authors by the 1988 revision of *AACR2* could produce similar results. Machine matching can also be problematic with undifferentiated names and in cases where the same heading has been used for different entities by different cataloging agencies. On the other hand, some headings for which authority records exist will not be changed since they do not match a reference or fit any other processing algorithms. For instance, only thirteen of the twenty-four sample headings listed above match existing LC headings or references. Normalization and hierarchical checks resolve only four of the remaining problems. Clearly, machine processing alone cannot produce a clean database. Further research is needed, however, to determine the exact nature and extent of the problems associated with machine processing of different types of headings.

Regardless of the mix of manual and machine techniques used, the authority processing of the converted records should be completed as quickly as possible, given the dynamic nature of both bibliographic and authority files.[23] More importantly, the performance of the online catalog–and hence service to the library users–will suffer as long as the database is not under authority control. Planning must therefore include allocation of sufficient resources to accomplish authority processing of the converted records as quickly as possible. The interplay of resources and standards will also determine which of three approaches the library selects for authority processing: (1) performing all of the work in-house, (2) contracting with a vendor for all functions except loading records into the local database, or (3) dividing processing between library staff and a vendor.

Given a relatively small number of converted records, ready access to LC name and subject authority files, sufficient local expertise, and an online system with powerful authority control and editing features, in-house processing may be desirable for libraries seeking to establish and maintain the highest standards of authority control over their entire bibliographic database. Not only is the library free to establish whichever standards it chooses, but it also has direct access to the bibliographic items for resolving problems. In terms of the resources needed to undertake such a project, planners should not underestimate staffing requirements in terms of either expertise or numbers. Professional expertise will be needed with respect to past as well as present local and national authority control practices in order to develop project policies, solve complex problems, and to train and evaluate the staff who will actually edit and create authority records.[24] Sufficient editing staff will be required if the authority processing is to be completed in any reasonable time frame. Further, the local system office should be prepared to solve problems associated with in-house processing, including identifying the headings to be processed. This can be done by producing a list of all the headings on the converted records–in which case the same headings will occur more than once, with consequent complications for processing.[25] If the existing database is under strong authority control, "new-to-file lists" may be considered. Such lists would contain only headings that do not match headings already in the local authority file; consequently staff would only need to evaluate a given heading once.[26] Since use of new-to-file lists involves machine validation, the problems associated with this technique must be considered.

In-house authority processing will require access to the LC authority files. At present, these files are available from the Cataloging Distribution Service on microfiche, CD/ROM compact disks, magnetic tapes, tape cartridges, and, in the case of *LCSH*, bound volumes. Most libraries, however, will probably choose to access these files through their bibliographic utility on a record-by-record basis. Alternate access to the LC files may be necessary to account for system downtime or the inability of the utility's software to retrieve all possible headings.[27] Subject to local system limitations, libraries could purchase the LC authority tapes and have the local system compare headings on these tapes with headings on the converted records.[28] Machine processing limitations aside, this would be expensive, especially considering the low percentage of LC authority records most libraries will actually use.[29]

Ultimately, the success of in-house processing will depend largely on the capabilities of the local system. If the local system exhibits poor search recall or precision, staff will have difficulty locating the headings to be inspected. If editing capabilities are limited or difficult to use, a disproportionate amount of staff time will be devoted to manipulating the system rather than solving authority problems. At a minimum, the local system should have an authority control module with global updating capability, that is, the "capability to use one command to change all representations of a heading from one form to another form."[30] If a library intends to use machine processing, features such as hierarchical checks, reciprocity checks, and dependent field validation are also desirable. In sum, the more powerful the authority control searching and editing features of the local system, the more efficiently and quickly the processing will be accomplished.

The importance of the above considerations is demonstrated by the experiences of the University of California, Los Angeles (UCLA), with in-house authority control in connection with a series of retrospective conversion projects. These projects were undertaken between December 1984 and September 1988 and involved the conversion of over one million bibliographic records. Due to the number of records involved, a special project staff was hired to process the name and uniform title headings appearing on the converted records.[31] This staff consisted of one full-time professional librarian to develop procedures and manage the project, 3.5 full-time equivalent (FTE) paraprofessionals to do the actual editing and authority record creation, and .75 FTE student assistants to do initial searching of the LC name authority file on OCLC and manual entry of authority records into the local system. The librarian, Mary Dabney Wilson, began work on April 15, 1985, and devoted the next one and one-half months to developing job descriptions and project procedures and to hiring and training staff. Significantly, it took over five months to fill all of the paraprofessional positions, due to the specialized expertise and experience which online authority control requires.

Actual production commenced in June 1985. Working from lists of all the headings found on the bibliographic records converted during a given week, the student assistants searched each heading in the LC name authority file on OCLC and in UCLA's local authority file and then annotated the list to reflect the results of the search. The students made printouts of any LC authority records that matched or seemed related to headings on the printout. The weekly lists and associated LC authority records were next passed to the paraprofessionals, who searched each heading in UCLA's local system, ORION. As needed, they then edited the headings on a record by record basis. LC authority record printouts were edited in accordance with local practice and then returned to the students for input into ORION's unlinked authority file. As needed, the paraprofessionals created local authority records online. Under these procedures, productivity gradually increased as staff gained experience and procedures were perfected; but during the first six months of the project each paraprofessional processed on average fewer than fifteen lines of printout per hour. The number of unique headings processed was substantially lower than this figure, since the weekly lists contained each separate occurrence of a heading on the converted bibliographic records and the same heading could appear on more than one weekly list. To some extent, the same headings were therefore searched and inspected repeatedly.

Low productivity was not only due to the nature of the lists but also to the limitations of the ORION system and the high degree of authority control desired. Without a linked authority file, headings had to be searched separately in the ORION authority and bibliographic files. ORION did have keyword searching, but search precision was low since a "hit" was recorded even if the components of a search string occurred separately in different MARC fields. Bibliographic records therefore had to be scanned just to determine whether the retrieved record actually contained the heading in question. Since each record had to be edited separately, the possibility of introducing new typographical errors into the database was ever present. Initial standards called for the inspection of each heading and its conversion to *AACR2* form if this was necessary and sufficient information was available. Paraprofessionals were encouraged to do research to resolve conflicts or verify facts. These standards aside, considerable difficulty was encountered in processing corporate body and series headings, since it was found that many of these headings lacked corresponding LC authority records or that LC had not yet dealt with all the name changes associated with these headings.

Clearly, both procedural changes and system improvements were required if productivity was ever to reach acceptable levels. To this end, it was decided to defer work on series headings and to encourage the paraprofessionals to limit the amount of research they did. While efforts continued to bring all corporate body headings into conformity with *AACR2*, it was decided that this would not be necessary for all personal names. More important than these changes was the development of a linked authority control module for the ORION system. This meant that each unique heading in the bibliographic database was controlled by its own authority record. If a heading on a bibliographic record did not match a heading on an existing authority record, the system created a skeletal authority record for it. Editing the heading in the authority file also changed the headings on each linked bibliographic record. These improvements made editing far more efficient. Search precision improved dramatically as well, since it was now possible to limit "hits" to when search terms occurred in the same MARC fields in authority records. Some of these features were available to project staff as early as December 1985, with full implementation coming in July 1986.[32] The immediate result was a surge in productivity: lines processed per month jumped to 21.24 per hour in December 1985, and averaged 25.73 per hour in 1986, and 37.73 per hour in 1987. Further changes in project procedures emphasizing processing the lists rather than editing any heading that needed it helped boost productivity to an average of 65.99 lines per hour during the last nine months of the project.

Increased productivity by the paraprofessionals placed greater pressure on the student assistants to keep up. This imbalance was corrected by developing procedures for downloading LC authority records from OCLC onto floppy disks for subsequent uploading into the ORION authority file. This avoided having the students manually key the records into ORION, freeing them to concentrate on preprocessing searching. This capability also encouraged UCLA to add no-reference LC authority records to the local system and to change ORION displays to identify headings controlled by LC or locally-created authority records as opposed to machine-generated authority records. This enabled staff to avoid inspecting printout headings that had already been dealt with earlier. Since ORION screen displays now clearly indicated the number of bibliographic records linked to a given heading, it was also possible to establish a threshold for individual inspection of bibliographic records: bibliographic records were inspected for variant usage only if the heading in question was linked to more than three bibliographic records.

The presence of references in ORION's linked authority file meant that it was possible to have the system compare headings on incoming bibliographic records with existing headings and to generate error reports listing any headings that matched a "see" reference. This capability also allowed UCLA to shift from weekly lists containing all headings on converted records to "new-to-file" lists limited to headings not previously found in the database, regardless of whether the records were generated by current cataloging or retrospective conversion. This change obviously broadened the project's scope, although, in any event, work on these lists did not commence until the project's final weeks.

Despite all of these system enhancements and procedural changes, productivity never exceeded eighty-eight lines per hour. By the end of the project, 812,959 printout lines had been processed and 136,740 authority records added to ORION, of which 20,463 were created by project staff. These are impressive numbers, but they mean that only 64 percent of all the lines received were processed. There is also the question of the extent to which the work done approached the ideals of uniqueness, uniformity, correctness, and appropriateness, especially insofar as procedural changes and increased machine processing resulted in fewer headings being investigated. In an effort to answer these questions, a random sample of 3,826 lines was inspected during the last months of the project. Judged by the strictest standards, 37.74 percent of the weekly list headings (not lines) inspected had errors of some kind, of which 35 percent were attributable to project procedures adopted to increase productivity. The error rate for the new-to-file lists was 23.4 percent, with the proportion of errors caused by procedures remaining about the same at 31.7 percent. Errors due to project procedures most often involved failing to make "see" references from variant forms of name for headings linked to three or fewer bibliographic records. Carelessness was judged to be the chief cause of the remaining errors, the vast majority of which were cosmetic. Only a handful of the errors would have affected access or machine match/merge routines. No "appropriateness" problems were encountered; but it should be remembered that by the late stages of the project most major corporate body headings had already been dealt with.[33]

UCLA's experience suggests that, with a well-trained staff, powerful online editing capabilities, and judicious use of machine processing, good results can be achieved by in-house authority processing, especially with regard to uniqueness, correctness, and appropriateness. Heavy reliance on manual inspection and editing, however, will leave more headings that are not strictly uniform in terms of punctuation, capitalization, and diacritics. Such discrepancies may or may not be significant, depending on the heading normalization procedures of the online system involved. More efficient use of resources in an in-house project will be assured if authority processing is delayed until the local system's authority control module is operational. This criterion must, however, be balanced against the needs of the library's users, since authority control delayed may mean access denied.

For libraries that lack the resources for in-house authority processing, contracting with a vendor for this service may be an attractive, if not inexpensive, option. Vendor authority services emphasize batch machine processing, although manual inspection and editing of unvalidated headings is also available from some vendors. As is typical for machine processing, headings are first normalized with regard to spacing, punctuation, and capitalization to increase the likelihood of their matching a heading or reference in the vendor's authority file. Other normalization routines may correct MARC coding and some typographical errors, expand obsolete abbreviations (such as "Descr. & trav.") to their full form, delete initial articles from uniform titles, and rearrange qualifying data for conference names in accordance with *AACR2*. Links are then established between matching bibliographic and authority record headings, while headings that match a "see" reference are replaced by the authorized heading from the LC authority record. Some vendors maintain their own files of *LCSH* subdivisions for hierarchical checking of subject headings. Such files also permit the global conversion of obsolete subdivisions and the deletion of cancelled subdivisions. Similarly, special conversion tables may be used to change direct geographic subject subdivisions into their indirect form. In cases where a single subject heading has been replaced by several new headings, special algorithms and/or manual inspection may be used to select the most likely replacement. Other batch processes may include hierarchical checks of name headings and automatic deblinding of references.

For headings not amenable to machine manipulation, some manual inspection will be required. Vendors offering this service may give libraries the option of having all unlinked headings examined or only those which occur a minimum number of times. Manual processing may also include creation of local authority records, although vendors usually will not change source authority records on the basis of data found in the client's bibliographic records. As required, vendors can supply matching authority records on magnetic media as well as printed diagnostic lists of unvalidated headings.[34]

There are at least eleven vendors to choose from for authority control services.[35] Unfortunately, there are as yet no surveys of these vendors in terms of services, costs, and effectiveness. Michele I. Dalehite suggests the following eight steps in selecting one: (1) identify vendors offering authority control services; (2) determine the services available; (3) select the services needed; (4) develop specifications and issue a request for proposals (RFP); (5) prioritize the specifications; (6) inform all library staff of the capabilities and limitations of the selected services; (7) evaluate the responses to the

RFP; and (8) select a vendor based on needs and budget. Particular attention should be paid to selecting the desired services and to developing detailed specifications in accordance with local authority control needs and standards.[36] After a vendor is selected, careful monitoring of the work in process is required. While vendors monitor the quality of their work, it is imperative that the library develop its own quality monitoring program in keeping with the capabilities of its local system.[37]

There are no detailed studies and very few anecdotal accounts of the effectiveness of vendor-supplied authority control. This may be because relatively few libraries have used these services as yet.[38] The Kent State University Library, which used Blackwell North America (BNA) to process 783,779 bibliographic records within a six-month period in 1985-1986, was generally satisfied with the vendor's performance, while noting that BNA supplied duplicate (but not identical) authority records for headings used both as names and subjects. Other duplicate records resulted from local input errors and from BNA's policy of not adding or changing birth dates in personal names.[39] The Florida State University Law Library also used BNA in early 1986 for automated authority processing and was likewise satisfied with the results. In some cases, however, BNA's combination of machine processing and manual review failed to change some headings and made undesired changes in others because (1) there was no matching ''see'' reference for a heading LC had established in a different form; (2) the LC authority record was inaccurate; (3) out-of-date subject authority records were used; or (4) Blackwell's editors made incorrect assumptions. Since BNA now subscribes to LC's weekly subject authorities updating service, the problem of out-of-date subject headings should not recur. While BNA did supply some incorrect or unnecessary non-LC subject authority records, most of the authority records it supplied were both necessary and accurate.[40] The cost of vendor authority processing, which has been estimated at between ten and twenty-five cents per record, is probably cheaper than in-house processing.[41] Despite the limitations cited above, using a vendor is clearly the best choice for processing large numbers of bibliographic records relatively quickly.

The third approach to retrospective authority control is to divide the work between a vendor and local staff so as to take advantage of the relative strengths of the first two approaches. For instance, vendor-provided machine processing could be used to resolve many common authority control problems and provide authority records for all headings that could be matched against the LC authority files, while manual review of unlinked headings could be done in-house. Having all manual review done in-house is probably more expensive in the long run, but the initial costs are lower than if a vendor did this work. In-house editing also spreads the processing out over a longer period, but this might be advantageous in cases where the local system cannot process large numbers of records all at once. Both of these factors encouraged the University of Rochester to favor dividing authority processing between a vendor and in-house staff along the lines described above. How much in-house processing is attempted will depend on the number of bibliographic records converted, the capabilities of the local system, and the availability of staff. The University of Rochester concluded that one FTE professional librarian and one FTE paraprofessional would be required for the in-house phase of their project (involving approximately 900,000 bibliographic records), based on the fact that their local system was limited to about 50,000 maintenance transactions per year.[42] The Westchester Library system (WLS) used UTLAS International to link headings on bibliographic records to headings in the local and LC authority files and then to review unlinked headings manually "so keystroke errors could be eliminated."[43] UTLAS then produced a printout of headings that did not match for examination by local staff. While pleased with vendor performance, WLS cautions other libraries using this approach that the large number of headings which do not match any LC authority record will have an "inevitable impact on cataloging workloads."[44]

Whichever approach a library selects in applying authority control to its retrospective records, it must be realized that this is just the first step in a never ending process. The addition and deletion of bibliographic records from the local catalog, as well as changes in the LC name and subject authority files, will necessitate ongoing efforts to maintain the integrity of the catalog. Such maintenance can be accomplished using any of the methods discussed above, although it would seem that in-house processing is desirable here given the more limited number of headings needing processing and the immediacy of the results.[45] Some libraries, however, may prefer to send their complete bibliographic files to a vendor periodically for updating. Sending only new bibliographic records for vendor authority processing is also possible, but may introduce inconsistencies into the local catalog due to the dynamic nature of LC's authority files. Also worth considering are the notification services by which vendors advise clients of any changes in previously supplied LC authority records.[46]

Given the limitations of both manual and machine processing, perfect authority control remains elusive; but the resources are available to achieve a degree of authority control that was unimaginable only a few years ago. Taking advantage of these new capabilities will require careful evaluation of the available options and of each library's needs and resources. Making these decisions would be easier if we knew more about the relative costs and benefits of the different approaches and techniques available. Available data suggests that vendor-supplied authority control is quick and fairly good, while in-house processing is slower but, with emphasis on manual inspection of records, may achieve better results. Combining vendor-supplied machine processing with in-house manual inspection probably affords the best combination of speed and quality, especially if local staff concentrate their efforts on headings not susceptible to algorithmic correction. None of these approaches is particularly cheap, but vendor processing is probably the least expensive. Regardless of which approach a library adopts, it is clear that a firm commitment to online authority control is necessary, both as part of the retrospective conversion process and on an ongoing basis.

NOTES

1. Useful guides to the vast literature on authority control include Larry Auld, "Authority Control: An Eighty-Year Review," *Library Resources & Technical Services* 26, no. 4 (October/December 1982): 319-30; Arlene G. Taylor, "Research and Theoretical Considerations in Authority Control," *Cataloging & Classification Quarterly* 9, no. 3 (1989): 29-56; and Holley R. Lange and Diane B. Lunde, "Authority Control in Online Catalogs and Databases," *Library Hi Tech Bibliography* 3 (1988): 1-10.

2. *Anglo-American Cataloguing Rules*, 2d ed., 1988 revision, ed. Michael Gorman and Paul W. Winkler (Chicago: American Library Association, 1988), rule 22.20. This code is henceforth referred to as *AACR2r*.

3. For examples of how libraries dealt with this problem, see Judith Hopkins and John A. Edens, eds., *Research Libraries and Their Implementation of AACR2*, Foundations in Library and Information Science, ed. Robert D. Stueart, vol. 22 (Greenwich, Conn.: Jai Press, 1986).

4. In a sample of name headings taken from the City College library (CUNY), Laurel F. Franklin, "Preparing for Automated Authority Control: A Projection of Name Headings Verified," *Journal of Academic Librarianship* 13, no. 4 (September 1987): 205-8, found that 92.63 percent of the current (1980-1986) headings and 64.96 percent of the retrospective (pre-1981) headings matched an *AACR2* heading, an *AACR2* compatible heading, or a "see" reference in the LC name authority file.

5. Edward T. O'Neill and Rao Aluri, *A Method for Correcting Typographical Errors in Subject Headings in OCLC Records* (Columbus, Ohio: OCLC, 1980), OCLC/OPR/RR-80/3; and Edward T. O'Neill and Diane Vizine-Goetz, "Computer Generation of a Subject Authority File," *Proceedings of the ASIS Annual Meeting* 19 (1982): 220-23.

6. It took about ten minutes to find these examples in the Clarion University of Pennsylvania online catalog.

7. The authority control features of the major bibliographic utilities are described by Arlene G. Taylor, Margaret F. Maxwell, and Carolyn O. Frost, "Network and Vendor Authority Systems," *Library Resources & Technical Services* 29, no. 2 (April/June 1985): 197-200.

8. At Rice University, Donald T. Green and Dean W. Corwin, "Retrospective Conversion of Music Materials," in *Retrospective Conversion: From Cards to Computer*, ed. Anne G. Adler and Elizabeth A. Baber, Library Hi Tech Series, no. 2 (Ann Arbor, Mich.: Pierian Press, 1984): 280, found that probably fewer than 10 percent of uniform titles in music records converted from OCLC were correct in terms of MARC coding and content by either *AACR2* or previous codes.

9. For brief discussions of the blind reference issue, see Joanna Rood, "Practical Considerations in Dealing with LCSH-mr," in *Subject Authorities in the Online Environment: Papers from a Conference Program Held in San Francisco, June 29, 1987*, ed. Karen Markey Drabenstott, ALCTS Papers on Library Technical Services and Collections, no. 1 (Chicago: American Library Association, 1991): 39-40; and William A. Garrison, "Practical Considerations in Using the Machine-Readable LCSH," in *Subject Authorities in the Online Environment*, 54-55.

10. See, for instance, Arlene G. Taylor, "Authority Files in Online Catalogs: An Investigation of Their Value," *Cataloging & Classification Quarterly* 4, no. 3 (Spring 1984): 1-17; and Mark R. Watson and Arlene G. Taylor, "Implications of Current Reference Structures for Authority Work in Online Environments," *Information Technology and Libraries* 6, no. 1 (March 1987): 10-19.

11. See Doris Hargrett Clack, *Authority Control: Principles, Applications, and Instructions* (Chicago: American Library Association, 1990): 67-82.

12. Michele I. Dalehite, "Vendor-Supplied Automated Authority Control: What It Is and How to Get It," *Law Library Journal* 81, no. 1 (Winter 1989): 125.

13. Elisabeth Janakiev and William Garrison, "Retrospective Conversion of Authority Records," in *Retrospective Conversion*, 303-310, describe conversion of a manual authority file at Northwestern University. They found that student assistants could convert twenty to twenty-five records per hour.

14. Alva Theresa Stone, "Vendor Processing and Local Authority File Development," *Law Library Journal* 81, no. 1 (Winter 1989): 138, discusses use of an OCLC/NOTIS interface for this purpose.

15. See below, p. 14.

16. Agnes M. Grady, "Online Maintenance Features of Authority Files: A Survey of Vendors and In-house Systems," *Information Technology and Libraries* 7, no. 1 (March 1988): 54, reports that 76 percent of the systems surveyed used the MARC authorities format.

17. Jeanne Somers, "Blackwell North America (BNA)," in *Choosing a Bibliographic Utility*, ed. Leslie R. Morris (New York: Neal-Schuman Publishers, 1989): 91, reports on difficulties loading vendor authority tapes due to a problem in the local system software.

18. Grady, "Online Maintenance Features of Authority Files," 51-55; Taylor, Maxwell, and Frost, "Network and Vendor Authority Systems," 200-202; and Sarah Hager Johnston, "Current Offerings in Automated Authority Control: A Survey of Vendors," *Information Technology and Libraries* 8, no. 3 (September 1989): 236-64, discuss the various features available in automated authority control systems.

19. A. H. Clough, "Duty" (1841); quoted in John Fowles, *The French Lieutenant's Woman* (Boston: Little, Brown and Company, 1969): 82.

20. G. A. D., "What's Authority Control? or, The Tale of the Virgin vs. the Material Girl," *Library Journal* 115, no. 16 (1 October 1990): 45.

21. See, for example, Green and Corwin, "Retrospective Conversion of Music Materials," 280-82, who discuss OCLC's December 1980 attempt to bring music uniform titles into conformity with *AACR2*.

22. *AACR2r*, rule 24.1C1.

23. Elaine Peterson and Bonnie Johnson, "Is Authority Updating Worth the Price?" *Technicalities* 10, no. 5 (May 1990): 15, report that a three-year delay in loading authority records into their local system left nearly 25 percent of the authority records without a bibliographic record with which to link.

24. Job descriptions for both professional and paraprofessional authority positions can be found in *Automated Authority Control in ARL Libraries*, ed. Stefanie A. Wittenbach, SPEC Kit, 156 (Washington, D.C.: Association of Research Libraries, Office of Management Services, 1989): 7-34.

25. Marie Bednar, "Quality Control Measures Related to the Clerical Role in Online Cataloging and Retrospective Conversion," in *Second National Conference on Integrated Online Systems: Proceedings, September 13 and 14, 1984, Atlanta, Georgia*, ed. David C. Genaway (Canfield, Ohio: Genaway & Associates, 1984); 154, describes the use of such lists in conjunction with a manual authority file at Pennsylvania State University.

26. Jay H. Lambrecht, "Reviving a Retrospective Conversion Project: Strategies to Complete the Task," *College & Research Libraries* 51 (January 1990): 31.

27. The OCLC system, for example, cannot display authority records if a search retrieves more than six hundred records. OCLC Online Computer Library Center, *Authorities User Guide* (Dublin, Ohio: OCLC Online Computer Library Center, 1990): 3.3.

28. This approach was used by the Ohio State University. See Lorene E. Ludy, "LC Name Authority Tapes Used by Ohio State University Libraries," *Information Technology and Libraries* 3, no. 1 (March 1984): 69-71; and Lorene E. Ludy, "OSU Libraries' Use of Library of Congress Subject Authorities File," *Information Technology and Libraries* 4, no. 2 (June 1985): 155-60. Janakiev and Garrison, "Retrospective Conversion of Authority Records," 305, considered this option in 1981, but found usable LC name authority records for no more than 10 percent of the headings in their manual name authority file.

29. Library of Congress, Cataloging Distribution Service, *The Complete Catalog* (Washington, D.C.: Library of Congress, Cataloging Distribution Service, 1991): 33, prices annual subscriptions to the name and subject authorities at $11,595 and $3,280 respectively. The retrospective files cost $10,140 for names and $1,440 for subjects.

30. Grady, "Online Maintenance Features of Authority Files," 52.

31. Additional staff was also hired to process subject headings generated by current cataloging as well as by the retrospective conversion project. Since their activities were more fully integrated into UCLA's regular workflow, they will not be discussed here.

32. ORION's authority control features are described by George E. Gibbs and Diane Bisom, "Creating an Interactive Authority File for Names in the UCLA ORION System: Specifications and Decisions," *Cataloging & Classification Quarterly* 9, no. 3 (1989): 153-69. See also James Fayollat and Elizabeth Coles, "Database Management Principles of the UCLA Library's Orion System," *Information Technology and Libraries* 6, no. 2 (June 1987): 102-115.

33. This account is based on reports and memoranda by Mary Dabney Wilson and the author and on information supplied by Arline Zuckerman, Head of the Authority Section in UCLA's University Research Library.

34. This summary of vendor-supplied authority control services is based in part on sales literature from Library Technologies, Inc., Library Systems & Services, Inc., Western Library Network, Marcive, Inc., CLSI, Inc., Brodart Automation, and Blackwell North America, Inc. Blackwell North America's authority services are also described by Dan Miller, "Authority Control in the Retrospective Conversion Process," *Information Technology and Libraries* 3, no. 3 (September 1984): 286-92. Rood, "Practical Considerations in Dealing with LCSH-mr," 31-40, discusses UTLAS' capabilities with respect to subject headings. See also Dalehite, "Vendor-Supplied Authority Control," 120-23; Taylor, Maxwell, and Frost, "Network and Vendor Authority Systems," 196-97; and University of Rochester, Authority Control Task Force, "Components of Machine Review and Manual

Review When Processing Tapes for Authority Control,'' in *Automated Authority Control in ARL Libraries*: 58-59.

35. These include Auto-Graphics, Inc., Blackwell North America, Inc., Brodart Automation, CLSI, Inc., EKI, Inc., Library Technologies, Inc., Library Systems & Services, Inc., Marcive, Inc., SOLINET, UTLAS International, and Western Library Network. This list was compiled from vendor literature available to the author and by scanning both the product and supplier directories of "1992 Sourcebook," *Library Journal* 116, no. 20 (2 December 1991).

36. Dalehite, "Vendor-Supplied Automated Authority Control," 124-127.

37. Derry C. Juneja, "Quality Control in Data Conversion," *Library Resources & Technical Services* 31, no. 2 (April/June 1987): 156-57.

38. According to Stefanie A. Wittenbach, *Automated Authority Control in ARL Libraries*, SPEC Flyer, 156 (Washington, D.C.: Association for Research Libraries, Office of Management Services, 1989): [2], "very few libraries use an outside vendor to process the machine-readable database against LC authority records heading clean-up."

39. Somers, "Blackwell North America," 85-96.

40. Stone, "Vendor Processing and Local Authority File Development," 131-141.

41. Joseph R. Matthews, "The Problems Behind Retrospective Conversion," in "Retrospective Conversion: Issues and Perspectives," ed. John Drabenstott, *Library Hi Tech* 4, no. 2 (Summer 1986): 109-10. Stone, "Vendor Processing and Local Authority File Development," 140, reports that BNA's services cost the Florida State University Law Library about 11.1 cents per bibliographic record. The University of Rochester, Authority Control Task Force, "Final Report," 13 October 1987, in *Automated Authority Control in ARL Libraries*: 49, found that vendor processing would cost more initially but less in the long run.

42. University of Rochester, Authority Control Task Force, "Final Report," 46-54.

43. Maurice J. Freedman and Beverly Harris, "Utlas," in *Choosing a Bibliographic Utility*, 51.

44. Ibid., 52.

45. Stone, "Vendor Processing and Local Authority File Development," 137-39, describes maintenance procedures at the Florida State University Law Library. *Automated Authority Control in ARL Libraries*, 37-88, reproduces authority control procedural documents from various libraries.

46. Dalehite, "Vendor-Supplied Authority Control," 123-24, discusses different types of vendor updating services, while Peterson and Johnson, "Is Authority Updating Worth the Price?" 15, consider the desirability of such updating.